HERO⊙

of

HER⊙ES

HERO

of

HEROES

SEEING CHRIST
IN THE BEATITUDES

IAIN M. DUGUID

P&R PUBLISHING
P.O. BOX 817 • PHILLIPSBURG • NEW JERSEY 08865-0817

Page design by Tobias Design
Typesetting by Michelle Feaster

Printed in the United States of America

Library of Congress Cataloging-in-Publication Data

Duguid, Iain M.
    Hero of heroes : seeing Christ in the Beatitudes / Iain M. Duguid.
        p. cm.
    Includes bibliographical references and index.
    ISBN 0-87552-177-0
    1. Beatitudes. I. Title.

BT382.D84 2001
241.5'3—dc21

                                                    00-049174

CONTENTS

ACKNOWLEDGMENTS

No book is written in a vacuum, and I am reminded, every time I sit down to write, of the debt I owe to many people who have contributed to my thinking. This material originated as sermons preached in Redeemer Presbyterian Church, Oxford, England, and has been revised several times since then. Thanks are due to God's people at Mount Salus Presbyterian Church, Clinton, Mississippi; New Life Presbyterian Church, Escondido, California; and North City Presbyterian Church, Poway, California—for providing willing ears to hear the explanation of God's Word. The book itself has benefited from the insightful editing and comments of Maria denBoer and Thom Notaro, for which I am extremely grateful.

This book is dedicated to my wife, Barbara, my faithful friend and constant companion, who is never too busy to sit down and share a cup of coffee with me. That is no mean feat while juggling the demands of being mother, teacher, mentor, and friend to our five children, Jamie, Sam, Hannah, Robbie, and Rosie, as well as being a working woman and a showcase of grace in her own right. I can identify readily and joyfully with the Proverbs 31 husband. Thank you!

INTRODUCTION

THE CHRISTIAN HERO

It has been said that Britain and America are two countries divided by a common language. From my own unique perspective as a British person married to an American, I would say that language is one of the least of the differences. Certainly, we have different items of clothing in mind when we talk about pants, but the more British people know about America—and the more Americans know about Britain—the more you come to realize that the two countries have fundamentally different ways of thinking about things. We think differently about money, about politics, about opportunity . . . about so many different things.

What happens when you move from one country to the other is that all of your beliefs and ideas are challenged. You have to think again about all the things you do and the way you do them, because now you are faced with a culture that embodies a whole new set of attitudes.

That is also what happens when someone becomes a Christian. Christians have an entirely different set of attitudes from those of the general public around them. They have a different scale of values. They have different heroes. They are different people. Christians, however, are—or at least ought to be—even more different from other people than the British are from the Americans. They are called to march to the beat of an entirely different drum.

In Matthew 5–7, the portion of Matthew's gospel that is often called the Sermon on the Mount, we hear that drumbeat. This section of the Bible has sometimes been described as the "manifesto of God's kingdom." In it, Jesus spells out the attitudes that are to shape us as Christians. It is not intended to be a set of rules and regulations with which to measure ourselves and others to see whether we are good enough to be in the kingdom. Rather, as those who have been brought into God's kingdom, it is a call to our hearts and to our minds to be shaped by the reality of who we are as Christians.

The Sermon on the Mount challenges us with this question: "To which drum are we marching?" Are we marching to the drum of the world, like those around us, or are we marching to the drum of God's kingdom as we hear it in God's Word, the Bible?

Jesus starts his kingdom manifesto by describing the Christian hero (Matt. 5:1–12). In these verses, which are sometimes called the "Beatitudes" because they all start with the word "Blessed," Jesus paints a word picture of the person we are to envy. That's really what the word "blessed" means: it means that this is the kind of person we are to envy. This is the kind of person we are to be like. We all have our heroes. Some of us would love to be able to play baseball like Sammy Sosa, or to dance like Fred Astaire, or to sing like Celine Dion. Some of us would like to be rich and beautiful, or perhaps we would settle for being rich *or* beautiful.

We all have heroes in our hearts. We all have people we wish that we were more like. Maybe we know we could never be entirely like our heroes, but we want at least to be more like them. So we spend hours throwing a baseball around the yard or singing in front of the mirror, or playing the lottery, or shopping for the clothes that make us look our best.

Nor does this human trait disappear as we grow older. As we get older, and we start to realize that many of our dreams can never come true in our own life, we transfer them to our children. Instead of dreaming about ourselves, now we dream that our offspring will be rich or beautiful or play baseball for the Cubs or sing to packed audiences . . . or all of the above. We long for our children to live out our fantasies.

Now it is entirely natural for us to have heroes. It is part of who we are as human beings to have dreams and aspirations, to want the very best for ourselves and for our children. But Jesus turns upside down our definition of what a hero is. Jesus challenges our dreams and desires. He wants us to long to be a different kind of person. He doesn't want us to spend our time wishing that we were rich, beautiful, talented, and influential, but rather that we were poor in spirit, a mourner, meek, hungering and thirsting after righteousness, merciful, and so on. These are the virtues we are to long to see not only in our own lives, but also in the lives of our children.

This is, of course, radically different from what we are like by nature. How much of our time is spent daydreaming about becoming poorer in spirit or purer in heart, or more merciful or a better peacemaker? That is not the normal focus of my dreams! The attitudes of God's kingdom certainly do march to a different drumbeat from our natural rhythms.

In this little book, we'll be looking at the attributes and the attitudes of the Christian hero. What are the marks of such a person? What are Christians to long to be like? What kind of people should we set our hearts on becoming?

Jesus lays down eight attitudes that we are to have. These are not tasks we can do and then check off on a little list. They are defining characteristics, heart habits that mark the core of our being. These Beatitudes are the "attitudes" we are to "be." However, Jesus doesn't simply describe for us in abstract terms what a Christian hero ought to look like. His description has power because he himself came and lived out all of these attributes for us. He has shown us in living, breathing flesh what we ought to be, and what a faithful Christian should look like.

But Jesus is not simply a good role model to follow. He himself has completed the course in our place. For us who are Christians, his perfection is already attributed to our account, exactly as if it were our own. Studying the Beatitudes is not, therefore, simply an exercise in self-criticism, in which we mentally beat ourselves up for not being what we ought to be. Studying the attributes of the Christian hero will lead us to praise over and over again as we see how these very virtues are on display in the person of Jesus.

By grace, all of these virtues are even now attributed to every Christian's account; by grace, all of these attributes will ultimately be evidenced in our own hearts through the sanctifying work of the Holy Spirit. Here we may only make small beginnings toward imitating our perfect model, but thanks be to God that he will not give up on us until every one of his people is a perfect reflection of the Christian hero!

For Further Reflection

1. How do you find yourself being influenced by the drumbeat of the world?
2. What attitudes does the world think of when it thinks about Christians? To what extent are these an accurate description?
3. In what ways are the Christians you know distinctively different from those who aren't Christians?
4. Do you have a "Christian hero"—someone who has had a significant impact on your Christian walk? What was it about him or her that impressed you?
5. Why is it important that Jesus is not just our role model?

ONE

༺ஓ

THE POOR IN SPIRIT

Blessed are the poor in spirit, for theirs
is the kingdom of heaven. (Matt. 5:3)

Jesus begins his analysis of the nature of the Christian hero by telling us that he or she is "poor in spirit." Being poor in spirit is not quite the same as simply being poor in things. Many of us are, or have been at some time in our lives, poor in things. We know what that situation is like and it's not much fun. But are we poor in spirit? What does that involve?

To be poor in spirit means to know that we don't have any resources within ourselves, and therefore we have to look to God for help and to depend on him.

NO RESOURCES TO SAVE OURSELVES

The first part of being "poor in spirit" is knowing that we don't have any means of saving ourselves. One of the first steps on the road to becoming a Christian is coming to the point in our lives when we see that our own personal goodness is not good enough to measure up to God's standards. Indeed, we come to see that our own goodness never could be good enough even if we were one hundred times better than the best person alive today. As the apostle Paul puts it in his letter to the Ephesians, "For it is by grace you have been saved, through faith—and this not from yourselves, it is the gift of God . . . so that no one can boast" (Eph. 2:8).

Christians know that they are not saved by their own goodness and hard work. They know that even if they turned over a new leaf every day from now to the next millennium, they could never measure up. If they are to be saved, it can only be by grace—by the goodness of Jesus Christ credited to their account.

There's a great picture of what it means to be poor in spirit in the story Jesus told about the tax collector and the Pharisee (Luke 18:10–14). Both men went up to the temple to pray. The Pharisee prayed like this:

God, I thank you that I am not like other men—robbers, evildoers, adulterers—or even like this tax collector. I fast twice a week and give a tenth of all I get.

Like so many respectable people, he stood there full of pride, thanking God that he wasn't a nasty sinner like all those immoral commoners around him. Especially, he thanked God that he wasn't like that awful tax collector over there, who connived with the Roman authorities to cheat and steal whatever he could from honest folk.

The tax collector, on the other hand, stood at a distance and hung his head, ashamed of what he was. He simply cried out, "God, have mercy on me, a sinner." He was poor in spirit; he recognized who he was before God and so, according to Jesus, he was the one who went away justified. He was the one who received forgiveness, because he knew that he couldn't contribute anything to that forgiveness. He knew that he didn't have anything to give.

The Pharisee, on the other hand, received no forgiveness. In fact, he didn't even ask for any. His problem was his pride. He was proud of his own goodness and of his performance relative to those around him. To be poor in spirit, however, means the death of all such pride. It means coming to God and saying, in the words of Augustus Toplady's "Rock of Ages,"

> Not the labors of my hands
> Can fulfil thy law's demands
> Could my zeal no respite know,
> Could my tears forever flow,
> All for sin could not atone:
> Thou must save, and thou alone.

No Resources to Live the Christian Life

But there is more to being poor in spirit than simply knowing that we can't save ourselves. To be poor in spirit also means knowing that even though we have been saved, we still can't live the Christian life in our own strength. It's very easy for us as Christians to fall down at this point. We view the Christian life as rather like learning to ride a bicycle. At first, when we were just beginning, we needed Dad or Mom to run behind us and hold the saddle while we wobbled about. But after a little while, we got the hang of it and zoomed off on our own. We say to the Heavenly Father, "Thanks for saving me, God, but from now on I'm off on my own. You just stand back and watch."

Maybe we don't say that in so many words, but do our actions not speak louder than our words? I know that mine do. When I pass over spending time praying in order to spend more time doing, what am I saying? I'm saying that what I do is what really counts; what God does is simply a bonus. I'm saying, "Stand back, God, and watch me go!"

Or when I try to run my own life according to what seems right to me, with no thought for what God says in his Word, what am I saying? I'm saying that I can run my own life very nicely, thank you. I'm saying "Bye, God! I'm on my own now!" How often do we act as if we know better than God and we don't really need his help? I know that I often do. To be poor in spirit, however, means total dependence on God.

Remember the illustration Jesus gave of the vine and the branches?

> I am the vine; you are the branches. If a man remains in me and I in him, he will bear much fruit; apart from me you can do nothing. If anyone does not remain in me, he

is like a branch that is thrown away and withers; such branches are picked up, thrown into the fire and burned. If you remain in me and my words remain in you, ask whatever you wish, and it will be given you. This is to my Father's glory, that you bear much fruit, showing yourselves to be my disciples. (John 15:5–8)

God wants us to bear fruit for him—much fruit. He wants to answer our prayers. But that can only happen as we remain in intimate touch with Jesus, dependent on God and his Word. Otherwise we will be about as much good as a branch that has fallen off the vine. And dried-up vine wood is not even good for making toothpicks out of. It is good for nothing except the fire.

Jesus Shows Us How to Be Poor in Spirit

No one exemplifies what it means to be poor in spirit better than Jesus. This is, of course, no surprise. Since he is the ultimate "Christian hero," we will see that he embodies the perfect form of all of these attitudes. He is therefore the one who shows us perfectly what being poor in spirit looks like.

Of all of us, he was the only one who did have the resources he needed for life within himself. He is the wisdom and the power of God in human form, the Perfect One. Yet when the devil came to him in the wilderness to tempt him, he didn't answer with his own words (Matt. 4:1–11). If anyone could have done so, surely he could have! But no, he answered each of Satan's snares by quoting from God's Word, the Bible.

Thus when Satan said, "If you are the Son of God, tell these stones to become bread," Jesus replied, "Man does not live on bread alone, but on every word that comes from the mouth of God," citing Deuteronomy 8:3. When Satan took him up to the highest point of the temple and said, "If you are the Son of God, throw yourself down," he replied, "It is also written: 'Do not put the Lord your God to the test,'" citing Deuteronomy 6:16. When Satan showed him all the kingdoms of the world and said, "All this I will give you if you will bow down and worship me," he replied, "Away from me, Satan! For it is written: 'Worship the Lord your God, and serve him alone,'" citing Deuteronomy 6:13. Why did Jesus adopt this Scripture-based approach to temptation? Surely it is so that he could be our model of complete dependence on God, of what it means to be poor in spirit.

Moreover, if anyone could have afforded to get by on a minimal level of prayer, it was Jesus. If anyone knew what was the right thing to do in every situation, it was he; surely he wouldn't have to wrestle in prayer for guidance? If anyone had the power within himself to live a victorious Christian life, he had it; surely he wouldn't have to plead with God for strength to triumph over temptation? If anyone had the presence of God continually with him, Jesus did; surely he didn't need to set aside special times to experience the reality of that presence?

Yet the Scriptures show us that no one was more dedicated to a life of prayer than Jesus. He got up early to pray on numerous occasions (Luke 5:16). He went away by himself to pray before crucial junctures in his ministry: before choosing the twelve disciples (Luke 4:42), at the Transfiguration (Luke 9:28), preparing himself for the cross (Luke 22:39–46). In his prayer life, with its expression of total dependence on God, Jesus was a model of what it means to be poor in spirit.

This expression of the attitude of being poor in spirit was also what led Jesus to be baptized by John at the outset of his ministry. John's baptism was a baptism of repentance for sins, and therefore John sought to dissuade Jesus from being baptized when he came to him, saying that he should rather be baptized by Jesus (Matt. 3:13–14). But Jesus replied, "Let it be so now; it is proper for us to do this to fulfill all righteousness" (v. 15). In other words, such was his identification with his people that he would even be their sin-bearer. Therefore, it was fitting that as their representative he should also undergo baptism, not for any sins of his own but for the sins of his people.

Jesus took that modeling of what it meant to be poor in spirit all the way to the cross. By nature, he didn't have to die. He is the ever-living One. Yet the writer to the Hebrews tells us that he chose to share our flesh and blood so that by his death he might destroy him who holds the power of death, that is, the devil—and free those who all their lives were held in slavery by their fear of death (Heb. 2:14–15). He brought himself down even to the point of death on the cross. Why? Because it was the will of God the Father to save for himself a people, and that could only happen through the death of Jesus. Jesus shows us what it means to be poor in spirit.

BEING POOR IN SPIRIT

What would our lives look like, if we began to be truly poor in spirit? To begin with, our lives, and not just our lips, would express total dependence on God. This would transform our prayer lives. Instead of the optional extra that prayer seems to us to be now, it would become the essential and central focus of our lives. We would start to act as if we really believed Psalm 127:1: "Unless the LORD builds the house, they labor in vain who build it" (NASB).

Instead of seeking "quick-fix" solutions to our numerous problems and the sins that continue to beset us, we would plead with the Lord to use all of our trials to draw us closer to him. We would ask him to use our sufferings to fill us with a sense of our weakness and our sins to fill us with a sense of our own unworthiness, and both to drive us again to praise him for our full salvation in Christ. When we are perplexed and lack wisdom, we would turn to him to seek it, both through prayer and searching the Scriptures.

If we were truly poor in spirit, that would be demonstrated in an attitude of humble self-emptying, of willing to be the servant of all for the sake of the gospel. Does God ask me to give up my wealth? It is no more than he has given up for me! Does God ask me to give up my comfort? It is no more than he has given up for me! Does God ask me to give up my reputation? It is no more than he has given up for me! There is no task too lowly he can assign to me. There are no wages too small, no people too ungrateful or undeserving of my help, when I consider that I am to exhibit the same attitude as Jesus. Instead of our natural tendency to want to lord it over others and to win their praise and admiration, we would be content to do the work God assigns us faithfully, whether or not anyone else notices and applauds.

WHY BE POOR IN SPIRIT?

Why should we want to be poor in spirit? Jesus tells us the reason: "For theirs is the kingdom of heaven." God's kingdom belongs to such people as these. What more reward could we ask for? God declares that he is willing to be our God, to be our king, to be our shepherd. What a privilege! The Bible says that he himself will dwell with his people, and he will wipe away every tear from their eyes (Rev. 21:3–4). No one who is ushered into his presence on that great day will have to ask himself or herself, "Was it all worthwhile? Was it worth the sacrifices and suffering?" God's presence will more than convince his people that heaven is worth any cost.

Elsewhere Jesus compares the kingdom of God to a great treasure, to a pearl of great price. It is such a treasure that it is worth selling everything to acquire it (Matt. 13:45–46). To be in the kingdom is everything. To be outside the kingdom is worse than nothing.

Given the great value of a place in the kingdom, it may seem surprising that the doorway to it is open to all. We don't need to be rich to enter this kingdom. We don't need to be powerful. We don't need to be beautiful. We don't need to be clever. It's not like the country club, where you have to know the right people to be invited to join. We don't even need to have lived a particularly good life. All we need is to become poor in spirit, empty in ourselves, so that we can be filled with the righteousness of God. All we need is to trade in our own filthy rags of righteousness, and receive the clean white robe that Jesus offers to all who come to him by faith.

One of our basic problems in life is that we don't think about heaven nearly enough. That's the reason why our daily dreams are filled with the wrong kind of heroes. Our longings and aspirations turn out to be full of this world and empty of the next. Jesus, however, calls us to march to the beat of a different drum, and to fill our dreams with eternal realities, not earthly toys.

This is not because everything Jesus promises to his people here is to be filed away for the future, like a savings bond that has to mature before it can be cashed in. It's not simply a promise of "pie-in-the-sky-when-you-die." If we are Christians, then we are citizens of God's kingdom right now, even while we remain here on earth. We can enjoy vibrant fellowship with him now. He is our God even now. We are his people even now. We may begin to experience his blessings even now.

However, we will not *only* enjoy God's blessings here and now. Nor will we even *mainly* enjoy them now. If that were so, we might be right to envy Sammy and Celine, with their vast endowment of the good things that this world has to offer. But for us as Christians the best is yet to come. The best of the pie does await the heavenly feast, even though we taste the appetizers here and now. What is more, the best is well worth waiting for. When all the earthly dreams have turned to dust and blown away in the wind, God's kingdom will still remain. And the poor in spirit will remain with it, rich beyond belief in the things that really matter.

So it is that we are to envy the poor in spirit and to become like them. We must become like them in not depending on our own goodness to save us—for we have none. We must become like them in not depending on our own ability to live the Christian life, but remaining dependent on God every step of the way. We must become like them in longing above all things to belong to God's kingdom, to be part of his people, now and for all eternity.

FOR FURTHER REFLECTION

1. Define in your own words what it means to be "poor in spirit."

2. In what ways does your life demonstrate a failure to be poor in spirit?

3. How does remembering the example of Jesus show us what it means to be poor in spirit? Why is it important that Jesus has been poor in spirit in your place?

4. What Christians do you know who have shown you more clearly how to be poor in spirit?

5. How does a focus on God's heavenly kingdom help us to be poor in spirit?

TWO

❧

THOSE WHO MOURN

Blessed are those who mourn,
for they will be comforted. (Matt. 5:4)

W e hold these truths to be self-evident, that all men are created equal, that they are endowed by their Creator with certain inalienable rights, that among these are life, liberty and the pursuit of happiness." So runs the opening statement of the Declaration of Independence. It is a high and lofty declaration of the value and significance of every human being under God. Yet many people, not just in America but around the world, have taken the last "right" and made it their life's goal in a way the original framers of the Declaration probably never intended. "The pursuit of happiness" has become a central theme in our Western culture—a "right" that seems to almost everyone around us to be self-evident.

The Pursuit of Happiness

In fact, we live in an age when, perhaps as never before, the pursuit of happiness has come to dominate people's lives. In all kinds of different situations, people are asking, "What's in it for me? Will this choice make me happy?" Nowadays, people regularly abandon marriages and get a divorce if they think they can be happier married to someone else. An unhappy marriage is considered more than enough grounds for making such a choice.

Equally, many people choose their jobs on the answer to that question. The first consideration in their minds is not whether this is a job that is honoring to God and useful to society, but whether it will provide them with job satisfaction and enable them to live at a comfortable level.

Indeed, a vast industry has grown up whose sole purpose is to amuse us and entertain us and take our minds off anything unpleasant in life. Most people would be more than content to have this epitaph written on their grave: "He had a happy life." In an age that wants above all else to be happy, our motto is, in the words of the popular song, "Don't worry; be happy."

But, as we have observed already, Christians are different. Our attitudes are not to be the same as those of the world around us. Our attitudes are not to be those which are "self-evident" to the average person on the street. No, our attitudes are to be those laid down by Jesus in the Sermon on the Mount. Here are the "attitudes" that we are to "be," the ideas that are to shape us. Here is the description of the person we are to envy. And another attitude of the Christian hero is that he or she is to be a mourner. Jesus didn't say, "Blessed are the happy"; he said, "Blessed are the mourners."

SPIRITUAL MOURNING

You can see right away how different that attitude is from the attitude of the world around us, which celebrates the pursuit of happiness. But what exactly does it mean to mourn? Who are those mourners who are blessed?

First, we need to start by making a negative observation: Jesus is not simply talking about acquiring a kind of natural pessimism. In my experience, British people tend to be somewhat more pessimistic by nature, while Americans tend as a rule to be optimistic. In his book *The Silver Chair*, C. S. Lewis described a character called Puddleglum, who was a "Marsh Wiggle," a half frog-like character who was invariably expecting the worst from life. His motto was to recognize that every silver lining has its cloud. Such a naturally pessimistic temperament is perhaps peculiarly British, induced (as in Puddleglum's case) by long exposure to excessive rainfall.

However, this natural pessimism is not at all what Jesus has in mind when he says, "Blessed are those who mourn." Mourning is not simply a matter of going around with a long face all the time, always expecting the worst. Jesus does not want to turn us all into Marsh Wiggles.

Nor is the mourning that Jesus is talking about the sadness

of loss or bereavement. Jesus certainly knew what it was to mourn for such a loss. He himself wept with Mary and Martha beside the tomb of Lazarus, deeply moved in his spirit (John 11:35). But the whole series of attitudes that Jesus is describing here are spiritual, not natural. He is talking about those who are poor in spirit, not those who are simply poor. He will go on and address those who hunger and thirst for righteousness, not those who are simply hungry and thirsty. So the mourning he is talking about is not ordinary mourning but spiritual mourning.

A Different Attitude
to Our Own Sin

What is spiritual mourning? Spiritual mourning starts with mourning over our own sin. When the prophet Isaiah came face to face with a vision of the holiness of God in the Old Testament, his immediate response was to fall down and bewail his own sin. "Woe to me! . . . For I am a man of unclean lips, and I live among a people of unclean lips, and my eyes have seen the King, the LORD Almighty" (Isa. 6:5). He encountered a holy God, and in consequence he mourned his own sin.

If understanding our own lack of resources to save ourselves is the first step on the road to becoming a Christian, as we said in chapter 1, then this realization is surely step two on that road: recognizing the fact that we are sinners, and mourning that fact.

Nor is that mourning over our own sin something that goes

away once we've become Christians. The Christian never says, "Well, now I've been forgiven, so it doesn't matter how I live my life." Christians continue every day of their lives to mourn the fact that they are sinners, that their life doesn't match up to God's standard laid down for us in his Word. As they grow in their faith, they will become more and more aware of how deeply sin touches every area of their lives, and they will mourn more for their sin. They come to realize that they are far more sinful than they ever realized, and so they mourn.

The reason why this awareness causes such mourning is that Christians understand what sin cost—and not just sin in general, but specifically what my sin cost. They know that each and every one of their sins was piled up onto Jesus on the cross. My sin was pounding the nails into his hands; my sin was pressing down the crown of thorns onto his head. My sin was driving his sense of utter abandonment by God. When we realize that, then the knowledge that we sin each and every day—through accident, through not doing the things we ought, and through our own deliberate fault—becomes something we weep over. Christians mourn their own sins and the heart attitude of rebellion from which all of those actual sins arise.

Previous generations perhaps understood this better than we do. Few modern hymns or songs match the depth of Isaac Watts's old words in this regard:

Alas and did my savior bleed,
And did my Sovereign die

Would He devote that sacred head
For such a worm as I?

Was it for crimes that I had done
He groaned upon the tree?
Amazing pity, grace unknown,
And love beyond degree!

Well might the sun in darkness hide
And shut his glories in
When God, the mighty Maker, died
For man the creature's sin.

Thus might I hide my blushing face
While His dear cross appears,
Dissolve my heart in thankfulness,
And melt mine eyes to tears.

But, at the same time as we mourn over our sin, we must never be plunged into despair by the fact that we do still sin. We mourn but not as those who have no hope. Even though we are sinners, we have great hope precisely because we see our sins in the light of the cross. Jesus' death was designed to pay for my sin, and indeed for every single one of my sins. They have all been taken care of at Mount Calvary once and for all. So, then, Christians neither take their sins too lightly or too heavily. Rather, they mourn over their sins, seeing them in the context of the cross.

A Different Attitude
to the Sins of Others

What is more, Christians are also to mourn over the sins of the world around us. At this point it is important to see that mourning is a fundamentally different attitude to the sins of others than the world adopts. Most people, when faced with the sins of others, adopt one of two positions. Either they condemn those sins, or they excuse them. When we are faced with a rising tide of crime in society, how does the world respond? The world invariably either condemns the criminals or excuses them.

Both of these attitudes find expression on talk radio shows. Political conservatives tend to condemn sin: they say, "What these youngsters need is a short, sharp shock. We need to build more prisons; we should bring back the chain gang; we should institute 'three strikes' laws, so that anyone who commits three crimes is automatically sentenced to life in prison. Let's make these criminals miserable." Political liberals, on the other hand, tend to excuse sin. They say, "It's not these people's fault; they come from rotten homes and they can't find jobs; we have to feel their pain and understand the reasons why they turn to a life of crime."

What is to mark Christians out, though, is a third attitude: their attitude is neither that of the political conservative nor that of the political liberal. Instead, they are to mourn and weep for sin. In other words, the issue that concerns them is not simply the behavior against society and how pragmatically that may be stamped out, but rather the fact that this behavior is an expression of rebellion against God. What they want to see is not simply a change in this or that outward behavior, whether effected by punishment or compassion. Rather they long to see a change in heart attitude on the part of the sinner, in fact, nothing less than a commitment to a whole different way of life. Christians long to see lawbreakers turned into those who love God's law, for they love the God whose law it is.

This is what troubles Christians about the lawlessness in society. It is not simply that lawbreaking makes society a less pleasant place for us all to live. Rather, it is that God's law and his name are not honored as they should be. So the psalmist says, "Streams of tears flow from my eyes, for your law is not obeyed" (Ps. 119:136). Is that how we typically respond to the sins of others? Do we weep for the fact that God's law has been broken and God's honor has been affronted?

Remember how Jesus responded to the woman who had been caught in adultery (John 8:1–11)? The conservatives, who prided themselves on being tough on crime, were eager to condemn her and stone her. The liberals, who prided themselves on their compassion toward the sinner, would have been happy simply to excuse her behavior. But Jesus' response fits into neither category.

Instead, Jesus replied to the situation in a very interesting way. First, he disarmed the conservative onslaught by simply saying, "If any one of you is without sin, let him be the first to throw a stone" (John 8:7). After they had all left, however, he then turned to the woman, declared that he also would not condemn her, and said, "Go now and leave your life of sin" (John 8:11). Notice that he didn't simply say to her, "Don't do it again"; he said, "Go now and leave your life of sin." His concern is much broader than this one act. By saying this, he was challenging her whole attitude of rebellion against God, of which her adultery was merely one expression. By saying this, he was bringing God into the picture and seeking to confront her with the reality of whom her sin was against.

So also we find Jesus lamenting over Jerusalem, crying out, "O Jerusalem, Jerusalem, you who kill the prophets and stone those sent to you, how often I have longed to gather your children together, as a hen gathers her chicks under her wings but you were not willing" (Matt. 23:37). He was mourning not simply over the wrong actions that were taking place there in Jerusalem but especially over her hardness of heart that kept her from coming to him in faith.

How often have we mourned like that over the sins of another, mourning not simply for what that behavior has done to us or to others but for the rebellion against God that such sin expresses? We are quick to lament when we are hurt by the sin of another, or when someone we care about is devastated because of sin. Yet how slow we are to lament and mourn any rebellion against God that doesn't touch us personally! We are ready to judge it or to excuse it, depending on our temperament, but not to mourn the tragedy of a life lived with something other than the living God at its center.

How Can We Not Mourn?

Moreover, when we look at a lost humanity, how can we not mourn? How can we fail to be moved by the desperate condition of so many men, women, and children, who live within a stone's throw of our doorways and yet who are light years away from a relationship with God? There are hundreds and thousands who are pursuing life, liberty, and happiness with great enthusiasm. They may be living in abject misery or finding a measure of happiness in life, but either way they are missing out on the one thing that really counts. They do not possess the reality for which they were created: a living relationship with the One who created both them and the universe in which they live.

Do we mourn over that missing center in the lives of those without God? Do we mourn over that absence of meaning? If so, does that mourning affect the way we live our life? Are we putting ourselves out and making ourselves uncomfortable, perhaps even foolish, for the sake of those for whom we mourn? Charles Spurgeon put it with graphic power in these terms:

> If sinners will be damned, at least let them leap to hell over our bodies. And if they will perish, let them perish with our arms around their knees, imploring them to stay. If hell must be filled, at least let it be filled in the teeth of our exertions, and let not one go there unwarned and unprayed for.[1]

Blessed indeed are those who mourn.

---

1 "The Wailing of Risca," *The New Park Street and Metropolitan Tabernacle Pulpit*, vol. 7 (1961; reprint, Pasadena, Tex.: Pilgrim, 1969), 11.

THE END OF MOURNING

But mourning isn't forever. We are not to mourn because it gives us some kind of masochistic pleasure. We are not to mourn because Christians are a naturally miserable, depressing kind of people, the kind who can see the cloud within every silver lining. Christians are not Marsh Wiggles. Indeed, Jesus specifically tells us that we will not be among the mourners eternally: "Blessed are those who mourn, for they will be comforted."

Mourning is a part of the in-betweenness of our present life. We live in between now and eternity; we are part of God's kingdom now, but we also live in a fallen world. We don't fit here, but neither do we fully experience the blessings of the world to come. But one day we will experience the fullness of the world to come, and then all our mourning will be taken away. On that day, we will be comforted. Therefore, we mourn in the present, but not as those who have no hope. We mourn rather because we have hope, but we do not yet see what we hope for.

One day our mourning for our own sin will be taken away, for we will sin no more. Isn't that one of the great things to look forward to in heaven? There will be no more sin! There will be no more sorrow over our own failure. There will be no more crying out, "Who will rescue me from this body of death?" (Rom. 7:24), for then we will once and for all be delivered! The righteousness that has been planted in us as a seed, which so often in this life seems to be bearing but little fruit, will then burst into full flower.

Does that prospect hold an attraction for you? Heaven is not the great retirement condominium complex in the sky with perfect weather and unlimited golf! It is not eternally enjoying our little earthly pleasures without the little earthly frustrations. Rather, it is worshiping God eternally in perfect holiness. If we indeed know what it is to mourn over our own sin, to hate the things we find ourselves doing, to hate the coldness of heart that we have toward God, to hate the freedom with which we pile transgression upon transgression onto the shoulders of Jesus, then we will long to be comforted by the complete removal of our sin.

Not only that, but on that day we will no longer mourn for the sin of others. At present, we live as aliens and strangers in a land that is not our own. As the psalmist describes his experience in Psalm 120,

> Woe to me that I dwell in Meshech, that I live among the tents of Kedar! Too long have I lived among those who hate peace. I am a man of peace; but when I speak, they are for war.

He knew that he didn't fit in his earthly surroundings. He was out of step with those who lived around him, because his heart's desire was different from theirs. He sought holiness; they sought their own way. He sought peace, and they were for war. On that day, however, that will no longer be the case. Then we will be surrounded only by those who worship the Lord, those who have been cleansed by him and who have been forgiven by the power purchased in his blood.

On that final day, the full number of the Lord's people will have been redeemed. We will see the great multitudes coming from North and South and East and West to join in the feast of the kingdom. At present, it may seem that those who are enlisted in God's army are but few and insignificant in the eyes of the world. It may seem that many more reject him or live without recognizing his reality and his sovereignty over them. But then, on the last day, we will see the full measure of his triumph.

On that day, perhaps, we will meet people who will say, "You were the first one who spoke to me about Jesus. I never forgot what you said to me once about his love for us. Those words stuck with me and now here I am with you." Oh, to be comforted with that kind of comfort! That we might see the fruit of our labors, that we might see the glory of God revealed and join wholeheartedly in the worship of Jesus—what a comfort that will indeed be!

JESUS, THE MOURNER

But that ultimate comfort is only possible if we join the mourners now. Jesus is our perfect model of all of these Beatitudes. He shows us what each of them means, and more than that, he has fulfilled each of them perfectly in our place. What did it mean for Jesus to be among the mourners? It meant that he himself had first to drink the cup of suffering before he could return to the Father, with our salvation in his hand, fully paid for.

Jesus had to experience firsthand the pain of living in a fallen world. He had to endure a place where things fall apart and loved ones die, where every rose has its thorn. Even the sinless One wept here on earth, not for his own sins—for he had none—but for the sins of others. Beside that tomb he wept with Martha and Mary for the consequences of the first man's sin, through which sin and death entered the world at large. The world was never meant to be this way! That is why we have no text that tells us "Jesus laughed" while he lived on earth, to parallel the verse "Jesus wept" (John 11:35). Rather, he was known as "a man of sorrows, and acquainted with grief" (Isa. 53:3 NASB). Jesus certainly knew what it was to be among the mourners.

But Jesus is no longer among the mourners. Now that he is enthroned in heaven, he weeps no more. Now the Lord laughs, Psalm 2 tells us, at the feeble plans of the wicked. All the plots of the evil one and his earthly accomplices can do nothing to prevent God from accomplishing his purpose. That purpose, on God's part, is to redeem a people for himself, a people of great joy. That same Isaiah who foresaw the coming of the "man of sorrows" also foresaw the consequences of his coming for his people.

> The ransomed of the LORD will return. They will enter Zion with singing; everlasting joy will crown their heads. Gladness and joy will overtake them, and sorrow and sighing will flee away. (Isa. 35:10)

Alternatively, as Revelation 21 puts it, "[God himself] will wipe every tear from their eyes. There will be no more death or mourning or crying or pain, for the old order of things has passed away" (Rev. 21:4).

However, that new order of things has not yet been fully inaugurated. Before Jesus could return to the Father's side, his work accomplished, he first had to become a mourner. First mourning, then subsequently comfort was the pattern of life for Jesus. If it was so for our Lord, must it not also be thus for us? But the pattern of Jesus' life of mourning gives us hope. We mourn in the sure and certain hope that one day there will be an end to our mourning, when we will enter Immanuel's land and dwell forever in God's presence. As Anne Cousin wrote in her hymn reflecting on the dying words of Samuel Rutherford:

The sands of time are sinking,
The dawn of heaven breaks,
The summer morn I've sighed for,
The fair, sweet morn awakes.
Dark, dark hath been the midnight,
But dayspring is at hand;
And glory, glory dwelleth
In Emmanuel's land.

The King there in His beauty,
Without a veil is seen:
It were a well spent journey,
Though seven deaths lay between:
The Lamb, with His fair army,
Doth on Mount Zion stand,
And glory, glory dwelleth
In Immanuel's land.

O Christ, He is the fountain,
The deep, sweet well of love;
The streams on earth I've tasted,
More deep I'll drink above.
There to an ocean fullness
His mercy doth expand.
And glory, glory dwelleth
In Immanuel's land.

Blessed are those who mourn over their own sin; for they will be comforted: in Jesus, the penalty of their sin is paid for and its power over them canceled.

Blessed are those who mourn over the sins of others, for they will be comforted: they will be granted a place in God's kingdom among God's people, where sin will no longer enter.

Blessed are those who mourn over a lost humanity, for they will be comforted: they will see the full multitude of the Lord's people brought into the kingdom.

FOR FURTHER REFLECTION

1. In what ways are you affected by the prevailing motto of society: "Don't worry; be happy"?

2. What does it mean to be a spiritual mourner?

3. In what ways does Jesus show us how to mourn?

4. Are there other Christians you know who have modeled this attitude well?

5. How does our present attitude of mourning make heaven more desirable?

THREE

✦

THE MEEK

*Blessed are the meek, for they will
inherit the earth. (Matt. 5:5)*

Hollywood heroes are always strong. They ride tall in the
saddle. They invariably shoot straighter than the bad
guys, punch harder, and win out in the end against all
odds because of their strength. That depiction is no coincidence.
It expresses a deep-seated attitude of our society that strength is
what really counts. Might is right and the weak go to the wall.

So when Jesus says, "Blessed are the meek, for they will inherit the earth," our society is inclined to laugh at him. It is an
old joke to revise the saying to, "The meek will inherit the
earth—if that's okay with the rest of you." People laugh at that
old joke and find it funny precisely because deep down we believe
that meekness is weakness and the weak will always be dispos-
sessed by the strong.

Once again, we see that what Jesus is saying in the Beatitudes is radically out of step with our society. His way is at odds

with the way most people around us think, indeed even with what we usually think in our heart of hearts. But as Christians, we are not to be shaped by what everyone else thinks. We're not even to be shaped by what we are naturally inclined to think. We are to be shaped by the attitudes that Jesus lays down here. Here Jesus is challenging us to envy the meek. In other words, he wants to re-shape our thinking about strength and weakness and then have that reshaped thinking affect the way we live our lives.

TRUE MEEKNESS

We need to start out by asking, as we have with all of these Beatitudes, What does it mean to be meek? Until we understand what the word means, we aren't likely to become living examples of it. What is meekness? Meekness has been defined as "a humble and gentle attitude to others based on a true estimate of our-selves."[1] In other words, to be meek we have to know who we re-ally are and then live on the basis of that knowledge.

Having looked at the first two Beatitudes, we are already some way toward knowing who we are as Christians. Christians are poor in spirit; they recognize that they haven't the resources to save themselves or even to live the Christian life on their own. Christians mourn over their sin and the sins of others. If both of those things are true for us, then we are a long way toward know-

[1] See D. M. Lloyd Jones, *Studies in the Sermon on the Mount* (Grand Rapids: Eerdmans, 1959), 1:68–70.

ing who we are as Christians. We are not filled with a belief in our own goodness and power but rather a sense of our own sin and weakness. That's a true estimate of who we really are.

Now knowing who we really are as Christians leads to two kinds of behavior toward others. On the one hand, we'll be free from defensiveness. For example, it is one thing for me to say about myself, "I'm not very good at getting things organized." But if someone else comes up and criticizes my organizational abilities, I still feel like responding in kind. I want to say, "Well, you're not so hot yourself." I get defensive. That's not meekness. The meek person is able to receive criticism, without getting defensive. The meek person is able to say, "You're absolutely right. That's an aspect of my life where I really don't do very well. Would you help me improve in this area?" This freedom from defensiveness characterizes the meek not simply when they are shown their character flaws but even when their sin is pointed out to them.

Where though does such humility come from? How are such people so easily able to receive criticism and rebuke? The answer is that it comes from knowing who they really are. It's not news to them that they are big sinners, so they can deal with others' pointing out that fact. They know their own sins, they acknowledge their own lack of resources, and so they are not destroyed by the knowledge that other people know too.

But if our response to criticism only goes that far, we may not be meek; we may just be weak. Weak people too are able to receive criticism without getting defensive. They don't say anything in response to criticism; they just roll over and play the doormat.

Perhaps they will say, "You're right! I'm just such a hopeless person!" In fact, some people think that they are being meek when they are actually just being a doormat.

How can we tell if we are meek and not just weak? We are being meek if we also have a second kind of behavior as well as the first. The second kind of behavior is this: we can stand up to wrongdoing and face persecution with boldness. Meek people are tough as well as tender. They have tender consciences to their own weaknesses and faults, and they are quick to admit their own mistakes, but they are also able to be tough in facing up to wrongdoing. As we are going to see in the next chapter, they hunger and thirst after righteousness. They don't bring out the big guns to defend their own rights and reputations but they will pugnaciously defend the rights and reputations of others, no matter what the opposition.

THE SECRET OF MEEKNESS

Where does this boldness of the meek come from? It too comes from knowing who they really are. For the meek know that even while they are great sinners, they are loved by an even greater God. Although their own sinfulness boggles their minds, so also does the grace of their wonderful God. Although they are far more wicked in their hearts than they ever dared to imagine, they are also far more deeply loved than they ever dared to hope.

Having been forgiven by this God and loved by him in this way, what does it matter what everyone else thinks? No matter how fierce the opposition may be, it is of no account. Having been loved this much, the truly meek person will endure any difficulty for the sake of magnifying God's greatness. A good example of such a truly meek person is found in John Bunyan's Pilgrim. As Bunyan describes him in his famous hymn,

> Who would true valor see?
> Let him come hither.
> One here will constant be,
> Come wind come weather.
> There's no discouragement,
> Will make him once relent,
> His first avowed intent
> To be a pilgrim.

It was Pilgrim's grasp of the gospel—of the weight of his own sin and of its full pardon at the cross—that gave him the passion and meekness to stand up to any opposition or difficulty.

Now most of us, if we're really honest, would have to admit that we are the exact opposite of meekness. We are quick to stand up for our own rights and reputation and eager for everyone to think well of us. At the same time, we are slow, very slow, to put ourselves out for the sake of others or for the sake of God's reputation. We'd much rather hear God's name taken in vain than our own.

The meek, though, have boldness combined with humility. They have the willingness to take on any opposition for the sake of God or others, while at the same time being equally willing to put up with any insult or indignity aimed at themselves. The reason they are able to do so is because they have committed their cause to God. This is the real secret of being meek. If we are meek, we don't care what others think of us. We don't even care what we think of ourselves. We only care what God thinks of us.

THE MODEL OF MEEKNESS

Boldness combined with humility: where better do we see these virtues displayed than in Jesus? Was he not the very picture of what it means to be meek? On the one hand, he didn't stand up for his own rights. Isaiah prophesied of him, "He was oppressed and afflicted, yet he did not open his mouth; he was led like a lamb to the slaughter, and as a sheep before her shearers is silent, so he did not open his mouth" (Isa. 53:7). So indeed he was.

Jesus was abused by the soldiers and flogged by Pilate, but he did not respond with a torrent of abuse. Having been all but silent at his trial, it was only when he was crucified that he opened his mouth. He did so then not to curse his oppressors but to pray for them: "Father, forgive them," he cried, "for they do not know what they are doing." The Meek One could bear any personal indignity at the hands of others, even to the point of death.

At the same time, however, Jesus was no weakling. "Gentle Jesus, meek and mild," could equally well take up a whip and turn out all those who had made a marketplace out of the temple (John 2:13–16). It was after that incident that his disciples remembered the Old Testament saying: "Zeal for your house consumes me" (Ps. 69:9). Jesus was passionate in his pursuit of righteousness, as passionate about protecting God's honor and the rights of others as he was willing to forgo his own rights. He was bold concerning others, yet humble concerning himself. That's meekness.

WHY BE MEEK?

Why, though, should we be meek? The reason we should be meek, according to Jesus, is that the meek will inherit the earth. At least, that is how it reads in most English translations, following the lead of the old King James Version. But the word translated "earth" has a range of possible meanings and could also be translated "land." In my judgment, the word "land" fits the context better here. For what Jesus is doing here is actually quoting from Psalm 37:11, where it says, "The meek will inherit the land and enjoy great peace."

Why is this distinction important? I think that "land" gets across what Jesus is driving at better than "earth," because most people would be very happy to inherit the earth. There was a popular song a few years ago entitled, "Everybody Wants to Rule the World." Likewise, the German philosopher Nietzsche once argued that the most basic drive in all of us was "the will to power"—the desire to rule the world, or at least our own little piece of it. It seems to me that wherever philosophers and pop groups agree, they are likely to have made an accurate observation! Everybody wants to rule their world.

Here is the point: We don't have to have any spiritual in-terest to want to inherit the earth, or at least our own little bit of it. But "the land" carries all of the overtones of God's promise to Israel. One of the things that God promised Abraham back in the book of Genesis was that he would give to his descendants a land to be their very own. Indeed, during the course of Israel's history they actually possessed parts of that land for some of the time. But they never possessed it fully. The fullness of the promise al-ways remained tantalizingly out of reach throughout the Old Testament.

Moses could not give the Promised Land to Israel, nor could Joshua. Even David and Solomon could not deliver the fullness of the promise, great though their empires were. This was God's way of showing Israel that the land that they were to be seeking was something more than a literal slice of the earth. They were pursu-ing a heavenly land, which they could inherit by faith whether or not they owned a large chunk of real estate in the Middle East.

The danger for God's people was always that they would be-come far more attached to the earth than to the "land," more tied to settling down and owning property than to seeking after God. The danger was that they would become self-sufficient and proud, deeply concerned for their own possessions and reputations but not at all concerned for the poor and needy. In fact, the danger was that they would become the very opposite of meek.

Do we recognize that danger? It is still present today in our hearts. We too can become more interested in possessing the earth—or at least a little part of it—than in inheriting the land.

We are very eager to have a rich, comfortable, easy life, surrounded by the good things this world has to offer. But that is not the way it is to be for Christians. Here on earth we have no enduring city; we are looking for the city that is above, the city that is to come (Heb. 13:14). This world is not our home, and this world's judgment on us is not what counts. What counts is God's judgment on us and the inheritance that God has stored up for us. As John Newton put it in his hymn "Glorious Things of Thee Are Spoken,"

> Savior, if of Zion's city
> I through grace a member am,
> Let the world deride or pity;
> I will glory in Thy name.
> Fading is the worldling's pleasure,
> All his boasted pomp and show;
> Solid joys and lasting treasure,
> None but Zion's children know.

INHERITING THE LAND

However, the meek will not invade the land. They will not overpower the land. They will not overrun the land because of their great might. They will inherit the land. It is God's gift to them, not the fruit of their own efforts. That is the way it was with Israel's possession of the Promised Land. They won the crucial battles not through their own strength but rather through God's.

They had to fight the battles, certainly, but they only won when God fought for them.

One of my teachers in seminary once described how he used to play "David and Goliath" with his little daughter. She would always be David and would be armed with a pretend sling made out of a blanket and a table tennis ball; he would play the role of Goliath. Her part was to move forward saying, "I come against you in the name of the Lord Almighty," and then to throw the table tennis ball. In response, he would fall down. However, she had to get her part right. If she simply threw the ball without saying, "I come against you in the name of the Lord Almighty," then he wouldn't fall down. Similarly, if she just used the formula and didn't throw the ball, he wouldn't fall down. Both faith and action were necessary on her part. It was exactly the same for Israel. Israel had to fight the battles, but the victory was the Lord's.

It is the same for us too. We fight the battles. We fight the battles against the sin that we still find inside our own hearts, the sin that we mourn over. We fight the battles against our own pride and self-centeredness. We fight the battles against the sin of others. We fight to protect the weak and those who cannot help themselves. But we do so in the name of the Lord Almighty, not in our own strength. We cannot conquer sin in our own strength, nor defeat injustice. Only what God does in and through us will bring about lasting change. We cannot overrun the land; we can only inherit it.

Nor do we inherit the land in full measure here. We may make progress against sin, but we will not see it eradicated from our hearts. However hard we labor for the rights and needs of others, we know that the poor and oppressed of the world will be with us always. Here we have no enduring city. We still look forward to the city that is to come, even while we do our best to see the kingdom established here and now. Blessed are the meek, who will indeed inherit the land.

FOR FURTHER REFLECTION

1. What is the difference between a meek person and a proud one? Between a meek person and a weak one?

2. Where does your lack of meekness show itself?

3. How was Jesus' meekness demonstrated?

4. How have you seen other Christians around you demonstrate true meekness?

5. How does the thought of heaven help you to be meek?

FOUR

*****

THOSE WHO HUNGER FOR RIGHTEOUSNESS

*Blessed are those who hunger and thirst for
righteousness, for they will be filled. (Matt. 5:6)*

When she's good, she's very good . . . but when she's bad she's better." So ran part of a jingle for the presenter of a program on a British radio station. If you think about it, that represents one fairly common approach to righteousness, doesn't it? Righteousness—or being good—is all right as far as it goes, but rather dull. Being bad is much more fun. Only the good die young, as the Billy Joel song put it.

This is a perspective on righteousness that the media pushes on us all the time in movies, advertisements, and magazines. What is more, it is an approach that seems to be gaining in popularity among the general public these days. Even though many people may not themselves yet live on the basis of this theory—that being bad is better—they have a sneaking suspicion that life would somehow be more fun if they did.

RIGHTEOUSNESS—AN OPTIONAL EXTRA?

The majority of people, however, still instinctively think of righteousness, or of being good, as being a good thing, provided that it is taken in moderation. They admire the idea (at least in the abstract) of doing the right thing. When asked about their fundamental philosophy of life, they will respond, "I try to live my life the best way I can. I try to keep the Golden Rule and do unto others as I would have them do unto me."

At the same time, if pressed on their actual performance, most people would also admit that they often don't do the right thing. What is more, frankly most of them aren't really all that bothered by that failure. So long as they haven't done anything really dreadful, like murdering people, surely a little weakness in the righteousness department is nothing to get seriously upset about. In other words, they don't think of righteousness as being an essential quality. To paraphrase the jingle: "When they're good, they are very good . . . but when they're bad, so what? It's no big deal."

Righteousness, doing the right thing, is thus viewed as nice but not essential. It's an optional extra. In essence, they are saying, "I do what is right when it feels good and when it fulfills me, when it doesn't inconvenience me, but let's not get carried away here. Let's not become fanatical about it." That's what most of the world thinks.

Sometimes, indeed, that is even what Christians think. We obey any of the Ten Commandments that suit us, as if they were the "Ten Suggestions." We do the right thing whenever we think people are watching us. But actually we are far more concerned about respectability than about righteousness. We are more concerned about our reputation among people than our standing before God, aren't we? Otherwise, it wouldn't make any difference who was watching, for God sees what we are doing at all times. Sadly, righteousness—doing what God has told us to do in his Word, simply because he says so—is all too frequently regarded as optional, even for Christians.

In this beatitude, then, as with the others, we come face to face with an attitude that not only contradicts how the world thinks, but it also contradicts how we normally think. Jesus says, "Blessed are those who hunger and thirst after righteousness, for they will be filled." In other words, Jesus is saying that the Christian's attitude is to be that righteousness *is* essential, just as essential as our physical need for food and drink. Jesus is calling us to get fanatical about righteousness.

After all, we're all pretty fanatical about eating, aren't we? We never complain about our constant need to eat. Three times a day, or even more often, we get a gnawing urge to eat something. So we do. We don't complain about the awkwardness of this appetite and ignore it or suppress it. Rather, we do something about it: we feed it. We don't call it fanatical to eat a decent meal three times a day. Let's face it, we're all addicted to eating on a regular basis. But nobody says to us, "You poor people; you're such emotional cripples, using food as a crutch. Why don't you give up altogether the old-fashioned notion that you need to eat and be free?"

Why doesn't anyone say that? The answer is because people know that if we don't eat, we won't simply get hungry, but eventually we will die. The same is true of all of our physical needs. We need food or we'll starve. We need to drink or we'll die of thirst. We need the air that we breathe or we'll suffocate. It's even true—up to a point—of our emotional needs. We need to have friends, people to whom we matter, or we'll shrivel up inside. We need to feel that our lives count; we need to feel secure, and so on.

What Jesus is calling us to see is that as well as physical and emotional needs, we also have spiritual needs that are just as real. Our most basic spiritual need is for righteousness. Therefore, we are to envy those who recognize their spiritual need for righteousness and be like them. Blessed are those who hunger and thirst for righteousness.

THE NEED FOR RIGHTEOUSNESS

Why do we need righteousness, though? It is easy to see why we need food and drink and shelter and air and companionship, but what part of us dies without righteousness? Quite simply, it is the part of us made for fellowship with God. We were intended to be God's friends and to be in close relationship with him, just as Adam and Eve were in the Garden of Eden.

But Adam and Eve made a mess of everything. Instead of choosing righteousness, they chose sin. Instead of listening to

God's voice and doing what he said, they listened to the serpent's voice and did his bidding. They chose to go their own way, to disobey God, and in consequence they were driven out of the Garden of Eden. They believed the lie that being bad would be better and paid the penalty of a broken relationship with God and the loss of life in all its fullness.

What is more, ever since then people have been doing the same thing. All of Adam and Eve's descendants have also chosen to go their own way, rather than God's way. As Romans 1:23 puts it, "They exchanged the truth of God for a lie, and worshiped and served created things rather than the Creator."

That group includes us too. I once listened to a radio phone-in program in which a caller argued that he didn't have to believe in God to do the right thing. Although he didn't personally believe in God, he said, he still tried to love his neighbor as himself. What he didn't see, however, is something that lies at the very heart of Christian righteousness. For Christians, righteousness is not simply a matter of doing the right thing; it is a matter of doing the right thing as an act of worship to the Creator God who has revealed himself to us in the Bible.

If we are loving our neighbor as ourselves because it makes us feel good, or because society expects us to love our neighbor, or because our parents would have wanted us to love our neighbor, then we are not doing it as an act of worship to God. We are doing it as an act of worship to ourselves, or to society, or to our parents. We are "worshiping and serving created things rather than the Creator."

RIGHTEOUSNESS SURPASSING THAT OF THE PHARISEES

Many people are proud of their morality, and indeed may be living remarkably upright lives. However, outward morality is not what the Bible calls righteousness, because the driving force behind it is not the worship of God. The Pharisees of Jesus' day lived remarkably self-controlled, upright lives. They fasted regularly, gave money to the poor, and prayed several times a day. But all that good behavior was not enough. Indeed, Jesus told his disciples later in the Sermon on the Mount that unless their righteousness *surpassed* that of the Pharisees and teachers of the law, they would certainly not enter the kingdom of heaven (Matt. 5:20).

One reason why the righteousness of the Pharisees was not enough was that it often was performed with an eye on the crowd. When they gave to the needy, it was to the accompaniment of trumpets so that no one could miss their beneficence (Matt. 6:1–4). When they prayed, they did so on the street corners, in order that all could hear their pious words (Matt. 6:5–6). When they fasted, they made sure it showed on their faces, so that all could admire their devotion (Matt. 6:16–18). They weren't hungry for righteousness, because they were already filled with their own self-righteousness. Yet since their acts of righteousness were done for the wrong reason, to build up themselves and their own reputation, they were thereby disqualified from being righteous at all.

Nor is this a problem limited to the ancient Pharisees. If we examine our hearts, we will all find that very often our "righteousness thermometer" registers a sudden upward shift in temperature when people are observing us! We too find ourselves disqualified from the category of the righteous not simply when we are being bad, but even when we are being good, because we are being good to our own glory, not God's. If we are filled with our own righteousness, we cannot be hungering for God's righteousness. We too find ourselves disqualified as surely as the Pharisees were. As the prophet Isaiah summed up our condition,

> All of us have become like one who is unclean, and all our righteous acts are like filthy rags. (Isa. 64:6)

So then we need righteousness, for without righteousness, without doing the right thing for the right reason, we can never please God. Without righteousness, we can never have the close relationship with him we were built for. Without that close relationship with God that only the righteous can enjoy, we shrivel up and die inside. But apparently even our best efforts don't qualify as righteousness, let alone the many occasions when we don't even try to do what we know we ought to do. What is the solution then? Is there no hope for us? We hear all the time of famine relief appeals for those starving for want of food. Will no one mount a famine-relief effort to save those who are starving for want of righteousness?

FAMINE RELIEF FOR THE
RIGHTEOUSNESS-STARVED

The good news of Christianity is that God has mounted just such a program to feed the "righteousness-hungry." He has provided for us a righteousness that is not the result of our own efforts. All of our righteousness is worthless. It wouldn't feed a hungry sparrow. But God has provided a vast feast of righteousness from which we are invited to eat. As Paul says in the beginning of his letter to the Romans, "In the gospel a righteousness from God is revealed, a righteousness that is by faith from first to last" (Rom. 1:17). Through what Jesus Christ has done we can receive righteousness, perfect righteousness, as a free gift.

The heart of the gospel is a great exchange program: all of our sins can be laid on the shoulders of Jesus on the cross, while his perfect righteousness is given to us. Paul further unpacks this great exchange in 2 Corinthians 5:21: "God made him who had no sin to be sin for us, so that in him we might become the righteousness of God." This gift of perfect righteousness in exchange for our sins is received by faith, which simply means by placing all of our trust in what God offers us in Jesus. Through that gift of perfect righteousness, our relationship with God is restored. As we trust in the death of Jesus in our place, for our unrighteousness, we are adopted into God's family, remade into God's friends.

But God's work with us is not finished when we become Christians and are put into a right relationship with him. That is where it starts, but it is not where it ends. For God wants to develop a new righteousness within us that matches the righteousness that comes from outside us. As we trust in him, therefore, he starts to work in our hearts something entirely new: real righteousness. We start to do things to please him. Indeed, we start to do the right things to please him. We start to ask the question more frequently: "What has God said in his Word about this?" or "What does God want me to do in this situation? I'm going to pray and ask him to show me what to do." In short, we start to develop a hunger and thirst for righteousness.

The funny thing is that having filled us with a righteousness that is not our own, we hunger and thirst to be filled more and more. It's like drinking salt water: the more of it we drink, the thirstier we become. So also the more we grow in righteousness, the more we become aware of thoughts and ideas and attitudes that are not yet fully placed under God's rule. The more we become aware of these things, the more we long for them also to be placed under his rule.

FEEDING THE HUNGRY

But Jesus says that those who hunger and thirst for righteousness will be filled. Now in one sense, we are filled already as soon as we become Christians. At least, as far as the legal perspective goes, we are. In terms of how God looks at us, the moment we become Christians we are filled with the righteousness of Jesus Christ. But we still hunger and thirst for that righteousness to be more completely expressed in how we live our lives.

The good news is that God's righteousness will one day be fully expressed in us! In heaven, there will be no more sin. There will be no more of the all too common experience of knowing the right thing to do, yet tripping up over the same sin week after week. There will be no more of the convoluted situations we now face, where it is so hard even to know what the right thing is, let alone to do it. There will only be perfect righteousness.

The telling reality is that most people in our society don't find that prospect all that inviting. There are probably hundreds of jokes doing the rounds, in which the punch line revolves around the fact that heaven is boring and people in hell actually have more fun. Therein lies the proof that those people don't know what it is to hunger and thirst after righteousness. If they did, they would find the prospect of having their hunger filled and their thirst quenched more appealing. In fact, if they could have all of their earthly hungers filled—their hungers for comfort, health, success, and wealth—without leaving this planet, they would be content.

Richard Baxter once perceptively commented that the difference between Christians and non-Christians didn't lie in their preference for heaven over hell; every right-minded person would hope to avoid the torments of hell. Rather, the fundamental difference between the two categories lay in the fact that Christians would not only rather have heaven than hell, they would rather have heaven than *earth*. For here on earth, we only experience holiness in part, and we only experience God's presence in part. Those who are hungry and thirsty for righteousness will long to be in the place where that hunger is fully satisfied.

LONGING FOR HEAVEN

We're back to thinking about heaven, aren't we? Each of the Beatitudes has left us there, thinking about what heaven will be like and eagerly longing to be there. This is no coincidence. Jesus wants us to be more heavenly minded than we are now and to think more than we customarily do about the kingdom that is to come. Yes, we can have a foretaste of it now. We can experience the pleasure that comes from obedience to God here and now, in some measure. But the best is yet to come.

Jesus wants a longing for that heavenly reality to shape definitively our thinking and our attitudes. He wants us to live with eternity in sharp focus. He wants us to make heaven the measure of our hopes and dreams, our desires and our longings. He wants there to be no moderation in our desire for righteousness, but rather a burning passion for holiness. Jesus wants us to long with all our hearts to be like him, to live for him here and now, and to be with him for all eternity.

Only God can give us that hunger. Our stomach for righteousness has shriveled up and died as a result of the sin we inherited from our first parents. We have no natural desire for God-glorifying goodness. But God can bring that appetite back to life, first of all by giving us a righteousness that is not our own, the righteousness of Jesus Christ. Through that gift, he can make us into God's friends, adopt us into his family. Once we enter the family, God then gives us the hunger for a righteousness of our own.

Do we have that hunger? Do we feel it growing in intensity,

even as we feed it? Do we long for it to be completely satisfied when our righteousness is complete in heaven? Blessed are those who hunger and thirst for righteousness, for they will be filled. Make us feel our emptiness, Lord, and then fill us to overflowing!

FOR FURTHER REFLECTION

1. How do the people around you display their attitude toward righteousness?

2. Who are the modern-day equivalents of the Pharisees? How does our own righteousness fall short of what is required?

3. What is God's answer to your need for righteousness?

4. How can you develop your hunger for righteousness?

FIVE

THE MERCIFUL

Blessed are the merciful, for they will
be shown mercy. (Matt. 5:7)

How different are we from the people down the street? In each of our studies in the Beatitudes, we've started out by comparing and contrasting what most people think with what Jesus says. Most people think it is best to be self-confident; Jesus says, "Blessed are the poor in spirit." Most people think it is best to be happy all the time; Jesus says, "Blessed are those who mourn." Most people think it is best to be strong and self-assertive; Jesus says, "Blessed are the meek." Most people think that righteousness is boring and unimportant; Jesus says, "Blessed are those who hunger and thirst after righteousness."

Time after time, Jesus is challenging the attitudes of the society in which we live. Time after time, Jesus is challenging us right where we live. So what attitudes does Jesus challenge when he says to us, "Blessed are the merciful"?

THE PROBLEM OF MERCY

How does that challenge the worldview of our culture? Which of us doesn't think it is a good thing to show mercy? Don't we all think that mercy is a good thing? The simple answer is "No, we don't." All of us, at some time or another, demonstrate our contempt for mercy. For instance, when we adopt as our motto, "Don't get mad, get even," we deny that mercy is a quality to be envied.

When people do something against us, how do we respond? Do we forgive them—or do we seek to get even with them? The temptation is frequently for us to say, as one of the Queens of England once did, "God may forgive you, but I never will!" Mercy, however, forgives freely.

To take another example, when we say about someone whose sins have come home to roost in their lives, "She's only getting what she deserves," we deny that mercy is a quality to be envied. Now it may, as a matter of fact, be true in a particular case that a person is getting what he deserves. All of our sins have consequences, and some of those consequences can be pretty awful.

The film *Philadelphia* gave a good example of this. In it, Tom Hanks plays a young lawyer with AIDS, fighting discrimination from his employers because of his disease. His employers have fired him because of AIDS, and the film shows us that there is no mercy in their hearts. There is no compassion for him as a suffering human being. They simply see him as someone who is getting what he deserves.

That's a very dramatic example. For most of us, of course, it happens in smaller ways. We may refuse to help people with problems because we think that they shouldn't have got themselves into this mess in the first place: they're only getting what they deserve. We may think that if we can make it by our own efforts, then so should others. If we can resist that particular temptation, why can't they? If they don't resist temptation, and they fall into sin and find themselves in difficulty, well, they're only getting what they deserve.

The Christian, however, is to be different in this area as in every other area of life. Our standard is not to be the standard of the world around us but the attitude of Jesus. Jesus says, "Blessed are the merciful."

TRUE MERCY

What does it mean to be merciful? First, we need to counter a wrong idea about what it means to be merciful. There is a counterfeit idea of mercy that goes like this: "Mercy means not being judgmental. What people want to do in their private lives is their own business and has nothing to do with me. So I would never condemn anyone." That's not being merciful, however; that's simply being soft.

That was the perspective of the makers of the film *Philadelphia*. They wanted people to come away from the movie feeling sorry for Tom Hanks because, after all, it's not his fault. He's just gay, like other people are straight. It's just the way he is. So he doesn't deserve to suffer from AIDS.

Now being soft is very common in our society. For instance, some people say this about young criminals: "You've just got to understand the awful background they come from. You have to feel their pain. It's not their fault." Indeed, when you are soft, it seems that nothing is ever anybody's fault.

Christians are never soft. They never say that sin doesn't matter. They have a true understanding of the way the world really is. They recognize that sin *is* people's fault and that serious consequences come when God's law is broken. They see the magnitude of people's debt to God. They try to help others also to see their debt to God. They mourn over sin wherever it occurs, whether their own sin or the sin of others. True mercy recognizes the reality of sin, and the fact that so many of our problems stem from our sinful ways of relating to one another.

But true mercy doesn't stop with a recognition of the reality of sin. True mercy goes on, and with eyes wide open forgives anyway. Christians are to be the most forgiving people. We're not to be soft, but we're not to be hard either.

The reason for that merciful spirit toward others is because, along with a true understanding of the world, we have a true understanding of ourselves. As well as being those who mourn over sin, Christians are also those who know themselves to be poor in spirit. Christians know that they are not getting what they deserve—not by any stretch of the imagination.

As Christians, we know the reality of what we deserve. We have all done things that are wrong against God and, as a result, we deserve death and eternal separation from God. Compared to that, even something as tragic and awful as AIDS is a relatively minor level of judgment. If we were given a single glimpse of what we would look like if we got what we deserved, it would give us nightmares for the rest of our life. But the good news of the gospel is that we have not got what we deserved. We have been shown mercy.

THE UNFORGIVING SERVANT

We can see what mercy means from the parable of the unforgiving servant. This is a story that Jesus told about a man who owed his master an enormous amount of money. Seeing that he couldn't pay, his master ordered him and his family to be sold to repay the debt. But the servant fell at his master's feet and begged for mercy, whereupon the master took pity on him and forgave him the debt (Matt. 18:23–27).

Now suppose that the master, instead of forgiving the man his debt, had simply said, "What's money after all? It doesn't matter. It's not your fault. Just forget it." That would not have been mercy; it would have been being soft. However, he didn't do that. First he showed the man the magnitude of his debt, and then forgave him all of it. Without recognition of the wrongdoing, there could be no mercy.

We are like the man in the parable, who could never hope to repay the debt and faced a lifetime of utter misery—but then, against all odds, was set free. We too could never repay God the debt we owe. We deserved the worst to happen to us, to be paid the wages we had earned, namely, death (Rom. 6:23). God certainly didn't minimize the wrongness of what we had done. He didn't say, "Oh well, it's not your fault. You really couldn't help it. It doesn't matter." That would not be true. Sin is our fault and it does matter. But at great cost to himself, God showed mercy to us, and so we must show mercy to others.

JESUS, THE MERCY OF GOD

In all of this, our example is Jesus. What did we deserve God to do to us? We deserved him to punish us for our sin. We deserved him to wipe us out with a snap of his fingertips and start all over again. What we certainly did not deserve is what God has done for us. He took human form in Jesus, with all its limitations. For our sakes, he knew tiredness, sickness, pain, sadness, and hard work. He took the form of a servant, washing people's feet, healing their diseases, teaching the disciples . . . and teaching them all over again when, as so often, they didn't understand it first time around.

Why did Jesus do that? It was certainly not for fun. It was not undertaken as an interesting experience. He did all those things for just one reason: so that he could show us mercy. He took on flesh so that sin could be taken seriously and dealt with once and for all, not just shrugged off. But sin was also taken seriously in such a way that our relationship with God could be reestablished. Sin was taken seriously, so that through his death, we wouldn't have to die. He suffered the agonies our sins deserved, so that we wouldn't have to.

Jesus knew that sin mattered. It mattered intensely, intensely enough for God to have to become man and die if it was to be paid for. He knew we didn't deserve him to rescue us like that. But he did. He showed us mercy. And as those who have been shown mercy, now we must show mercy to others.

What does that mean in practice? It means first of all that we must help the undeserving. The point of the parable of the unforgiving servant is not just that the servant didn't deserve the mercy he received. It is also that he should then have shown a similar depth of mercy to his fellow servant who owed him a trifling debt (Matt. 18:28–35). Jesus didn't wait for us to put our lives in order before he would come to rescue us. It was while we were still sinners that Christ died for us, as Paul reminds us in Romans 5:8.

Yet how often do we refuse to help others because they don't deserve it? Like the unforgiving servant, we do not measure out our forgiveness with the same proportion as we received it. We forget the vastness and depth of God's mercy in reaching down to save us. In Charles Wesley's words,

> Depth of mercy! Can there be
> Mercy still reserved for me?
> Can my God his wrath forbear,
> Me, the chief of sinners, spare?
>
> I have long withstood his grace,
> Long provoked him to his face,
> Would not hearken to his calls,
> Grieved him by a thousand falls.

I my Master have denied,
I afresh have crucified,
Oft profaned his hallowed name,
Put him to an open shame.

Whence to me this waste of love?
Ask my Advocate above!
See the cause in Jesus' face,
Now before the throne of grace.

There for me the Savior stands,
Shows his wounds and spreads his hands.
God is love! I know, I feel;
Jesus weeps and loves me still.

Our hearts are only moved to mercy to the extent that we remember and ponder the depths and richness of God's mercy. That is why it is good for us to share the Lord's Supper together regularly. As we see the broken bread, we are reminded of his body broken for us; as we share in the cup, we remember his blood shed to cover our sins. As we remember his mercy to us, we are moved to mercy toward others. Indeed, that is why many churches have historically taken an offering for ministries of mercy at their celebrations of the Lord's Supper. Such diaconal offerings are a tangible way of responding to the mercy shown to us so that the same mercy may similarly be shown to others.

DELIGHTING TO SAY YES

Responding to people's practical needs will often be a costly business, in both money and time. But however great the cost, Christians who remember the mercy of God will be eager to respond to the needs of the world through an expression of that same mercy.

There was once a commercial for a bank that showed a man on his way to work practicing saying the word "Yes" over and over with all kinds of different inflections and intonations. The slogan of the bank was, "We love to say 'Yes,'" and the man was supposedly simply preparing for his day at work. Like the man from that bank, Christians are to love to say yes.

We are not to say no to people's needs for help because of selfishness. We are not to say no because these people don't deserve our help. We are not to say no to the need because these people are ungrateful and will never thank us for it. For if we are Christians, we know that that's no excuse. We too were ungrateful and undeserving and unthankful when God sent Jesus to die for us.

Now that is not to say that we can never say no when someone asks us for help. Sometimes, the most loving thing we can do for someone is to say no. Sometimes people need us to say no so that they will become more independent and learn to do things on their own. A handout may simply increase their dependence on others or shelter them from the consequences of their sin in such a way that they are encouraged to continue in their sin.

Further, sometimes we need to say no because of our obligation to others, perhaps to our family or to our friends. There are times when we need to balance carefully our various responsibilities to people. But "no" is not to be our normal posture. Christians are those who delight to say "Yes" because they remember God's "Yes" to them in Jesus.

FORGIVENESS WITHOUT LIMIT

What is more, we must forgive others without limit. God hasn't set a limit on sin, saying that only people with up to a certain amount of sin need apply for salvation. God's gift of salvation in Jesus is big enough for everyone. It doesn't matter whether a person has lived a quiet conservative life, free from major outward blemish, or a wild life of sex, drugs, and rock-'n'roll. All of us are big enough sinners that only Jesus can meet our need for a Savior. His forgiving grace is not limited to "small" or infrequent sins.

Now if that is true of God's forgiveness, then it must also be true of our forgiveness. No matter how great the sin against us, or how frequently it has occurred before, we must still forgive just as God has forgiven us. Remember Peter's question that prompted Jesus to tell the parable of the unmerciful servant? Peter asked Jesus how often he had to forgive his brother—as many as seven times (Matt. 18:21)? No, said Jesus, as many as seventy times seven times. In other words, as Christians we are committed to forgiveness without limit, without keeping score.

How often, though, do we limit our forgiveness? We say,

either out loud or under our breath, "I'll forgive you this time—but don't you dare do it again." The merciful, however, hold out their hands to help the undeserving all day long and forgive without limit.

THE REWARD FOR
THE MERCIFUL: MERCY

What blessing does Jesus promise to the merciful? He promises them that they too will receive mercy. It may seem as though Jesus has got it the wrong way round here. Does he mean that by showing mercy to others I thereby earn mercy for myself? That can't be it. After all, we can't earn mercy. By its very nature, mercy can only be undeserved.

So what is Jesus saying? What he is saying is that, on the one hand, we can only be truly merciful—understanding the true nature of sin and yet extending love and forgiveness without limit—when we have received God's mercy ourselves. On the other hand, the merciful also know that their own need for mercy never ends. We can't extend love and forgiveness to the undeserving without growing greatly in our understanding of just how ungrateful and undeserving we still are, and how much we still depend entirely on God's mercy ourselves.

There is perhaps nothing that sharpens our appreciation of grace like learning to be merciful. As long as we are content to insulate ourselves comfortably from the needs of the world, it is possible to be fairly self-satisfied. It is possible to think that we are doing pretty well, so long as we keep our lives undemanding.

But if we start to go out into the world and attempt to show mercy—real mercy, not just helping family and friends and those who deserve it—then we will rapidly come face to face with our own self-centeredness and hard-heartedness and indifference. We'll be challenged by how like the unforgiving servant we are, who found it easy to accept great forgiveness but hard to give even a little forgiveness in return. Those who are merciful know better than anyone else their own need of mercy.

The good news of the gospel is that mercy is there for us. Jesus doesn't say to us, "Be merciful and earn your way into the kingdom." Jesus says, "Be merciful and know that there is mercy available for you too. In me, there is forgiveness to cover all of the wrong things you have done, be they few or many." What is more, it is a real forgiveness, based on a real dealing with those sins on the cross by Jesus. There is a real restored relationship with God, no matter what we have done or will do. That's mercy.

Many people, however, don't want mercy. They want to make it by their own efforts. They want to pay off their own debts to God through their own attempts at goodness. It can't be done. The only way to approach God is through his mercy. Those who come seeking it will find God's mercy is there in abundance, rich and full and deep and free. Those who know the depth of this mercy, will show similar mercy to others, helping the undeserving and forgiving without limit.

FOR FURTHER REFLECTION

1. Why don't most people want to give or receive mercy?
2. How does Jesus show us what true mercy is?
3. Think of three practical ways in which you could show mercy to those around you.
4. In what ways could your church demonstrate mercy in your neighborhood?

SIX

THE PURE IN HEART

Blessed are the pure in heart, for
they will see God. (Matt. 5:8)

We live in a world dominated by compromise. "Don't be so strict in your opinions," people are always telling us. "Don't see things as so black and white." Everything is simply a matter of varying shades of gray. Life, like politics, is the art of the possible. The nail that sticks out gets hammered down, as the Chinese proverb has it. Therefore, the pressure is on us to conform, to be like everyone else, not to stick out.

BLESSED ARE THOSE WHO CONFORM?

We learn this hard truth from the time we are children. At school, subtle or not-so-subtle pressure is placed on us to join in doing what everyone else is doing. If they are being unkind to someone, the pressure is on us to join in. If they are using swear words and bad language, it is hard to stand out as different and not do the same. If they are doing drugs and drinking, we stick out if we don't join in.

Sadly, it doesn't necessarily get better as we grow up. The battlegrounds may change, or they may not. From my years as an engineer, I know what it is like to be surrounded daily by clouds of four-letter words, filthy pictures, and mockery of God. Standing up against those kinds of things can make us extremely unpopular.

I found this out for myself one day during my seminary years when I was working at a hospital as a maintenance mechanic. I was assigned the weekend shift alone and, since things were quiet, one of my tasks was to clean up the workshop. In the process, I came across a hoard of pornographic magazines stuffed in a drawer meant for tools. Now since I'd been instructed to throw out the trash, and this was clearly trash, I threw it out! I imagined that I would hear no more about it. I couldn't have been more wrong! On Monday, my fellow workers, with whom I usually got on very well, made it clear that this was not acceptable behavior. My boss called me into the office and read me the riot act, telling me not to rock the boat.

I shouldn't have been surprised that my actions triggered this kind of response, though. That's the way the world is. The world says, "Blessed are those who compromise. Blessed are those who are tolerant of anybody and everybody. Blessed are those who don't rock the boat."

BLESSED ARE THE UNCOMPROMISED

Christians, however, are to be different from the world. The attitude that Jesus lays down for us is this: "Blessed are the uncompromised, those whose hearts are filled with purity." Once again, Jesus is challenging head-on the attitudes of the world, and also the attitudes that we so often demonstrate in imitation of those around us.

Why, though, do we need this heart purity? Why shouldn't we compromise just a little bit, the way the world wants us to? A few concessions would make our life so much easier and so much more comfortable. Is compromise really so bad? The answer to that question is found in Psalm 24, where the psalmist says,

> Who may ascend the hill of the LORD?
>   Who may stand in his holy place?
> He who has clean hands and a pure heart,
>   who does not lift up his soul to an idol
>   or swear by what is false. (Ps. 24:3–4)

Without perfect purity of heart, says the psalmist, no one can stand before God. Indeed, the Bible tells us that God's eyes are too pure to look on evil (Hab. 1:13). Only the pure in heart can be admitted into his presence.

So what do we really mean, when we say, "It would make life so much easier and more comfortable to compromise just a little bit"? What we are really saying is that what is most important to us is our relationship to the world and to those around us, not our relationship with God. The cost of making our relationship with the world easier by compromise is that our relationship with God becomes consequently harder.

We can't have it both ways. We can't be easy and comfortable with the world and easy and comfortable with God. Either our uncompromising purity will make us uncomfortable with the sin that surrounds us, and somewhat uncomfortable companions for those around us who want to be left alone in their sin, or alternatively our compromise will make us uncomfortable in God's presence. We have to choose whose esteem is more precious to us and then live in pursuit of that favor.

Now Christians, by definition, are those to whom God's favor is more precious than anything else. They are those whose hearts are set not on the approval of others, or even on the approval of themselves, but on seeking God's approval above everything. So I shouldn't need to labor this point for Christians: we see the need for heart purity, a heart free from compromise with sin, because we want to be able to stand in God's presence.

When one of the old Puritans was being urged to compromise and questioned as to why he had to be so precise in his observation of biblical standards, he responded simply, "I serve a precise God." If we serve a God who is holy and who values holiness—his and ours—above all things, then we too will want to be precise in our pursuit of purity.

THE PROBLEM OF OUR IMPURITY

But a problem arises at this point. All of us by nature lack the heart purity we need. Proverbs 20:9 says, "Who can say, 'I have kept my heart pure; I am clean and without sin'?" The answer is, of course, no one. No one is without sin. No one has a pure heart. In fact, quite the opposite is true. So Jesus says in Mark 7:20–23,

> What comes out of a man is what makes him "unclean." For from within, out of men's hearts, come evil thoughts, sexual immorality, theft, murder, adultery, greed, malice, deceit, lewdness, envy, slander, arrogance and folly. All these evils come from inside and make a man "unclean."

The problem is not outside us but within. We all by nature have defiled hearts. As I look into my own heart, that's exactly what I find there. I find the seeds of all of those sins in my heart. What about you? What do you think about when you let your mind run free? Are your thoughts naturally filled with whatever is true, whatever is noble, whatever is right, whatever is lovely, whatever is admirable (cf. Phil. 4:8)? Or, like me, would you rather not have people know what thoughts fill your mind much of the time? It is all very well to know that we need heart purity, but if we're honest we'll have to admit that we lack precisely the purity of heart that we need.

THE SOURCE OF OUR PURITY

So where are we to get this purity of heart? The Old Testament answer was to employ a professional substitute—someone else to do the job for them. We do something similar in other areas of life. For example, I'm not much of a plumber. I'm reasonably handy at a variety of do-it-yourself projects, but whenever I get involved with plumbing, it always seems to end up with large quantities of water washing around the floor. So if I need some plumbing done around the house, I call in a professional substitute to do the job for me. I engage someone who has made it his or her life's work to study the necessary arcane rituals and incantations, and who is able to make the proper sacrifices to the gods of plumbing. When the plumber has finished the work, sure enough, the water flows as it should.

That illustration provides an analogy for what the high priest did in Israel. He was a specialist, a professional substitute. It was his job to keep himself pure on behalf of the people so he could stand before God in their place. In later times, we are told that people went to enormous lengths to make sure that the high priest kept himself pure. On the night before the most important festival, the Day of Atonement, he would stay awake all night to ensure that he didn't inadvertently dream any sinful dreams. There was even a back-up priest ready, just in case of any accidents. Nothing was left to chance.

The problem is, though, that even such efforts could never make someone pure in heart. With enough trouble someone could be kept pure on the outside, but no one is pure inside.

However, the image of the professional substitute pointed forward to the real High Priest, Jesus himself. Thus, having described Jesus as our Great High Priest, the book of Hebrews says that such a High Priest meets our need—one who is holy, blameless, pure, set apart from sinners, exalted above the heavens. Jesus is the perfect substitute. His purity is complete, inside and out. He has lived the perfect life here on earth for us. What is more, now he stands at the Father's right hand interceding for us. In Jesus, we have been given the purity of heart we need. That's what the Christian message is all about: finding our purity, our righteousness, in what Jesus has done, not in what we do.

But as we saw in an earlier chapter, when we looked at the beatitude "Blessed are those who hunger and thirst after righteousness," God doesn't leave us in the state in which he found us. As well as giving us a righteousness which is not our own, he goes on to create a hunger and thirst in our hearts for a matching righteousness in our lives. So it is also with purity. As well as giving us a substitute, whose purity of heart is complete and is effective for us, so that by trusting in Jesus we can appear in the presence of God, he also creates in us the hunger for a matching purity in our hearts.

So in Psalm 51:10, David cries out, "Create in me a pure heart, O God, and renew a steadfast spirit within me." The need for heart purity was more than a theoretical concern for David. He has just been convicted before God of the sins of adultery with Bathsheba and the murder of Uriah the Hittite. He was well aware of his own lack of purity of heart. But he cries out for God to create in him just such a thing. So also we, as we find ourselves tripped up again and again by the sins that beset us, cry out to God for him to give us a pure, undivided heart, filled with loyalty to him.

GAINING A PURE HEART

But how practically can we attain a pure heart? We pray for it, but is there anything else we can do as well? That's the question the psalmist raises and answers in Psalm 119:9:

> How can a young man keep his way pure?
> By living according to your word.

The way to a pure heart passes through a life of devotion to God's Word. But this fact is true not simply because we find out from God's Word how we should live. To be sure, it is from the Bible that we find out what God expects of us. As Micah 6:8 classically states it,

> He has showed you, O man, what is good.
>   And what does the LORD require of you?
> To act justly and to love mercy
>   and to walk humbly with your God.

However, knowing what God desires of us is not enough. None of us lives up even to what we already understand of the clear teaching of the Bible on how we should live. Knowing the

Bible better may simply increase the gap between our knowledge and our performance. Unless something else happens to us as we read God's Word, we will be no better off.

Something else does happen when the Christian reads God's Word. There we meet with God himself. This is the other crucial function of the Bible. It is not only the place where we read what God requires of us, but it is the place where we come face to face with God. In the Bible, we find out what he is like and meet him for ourselves. We experience the greatness of his love for his undeserving people, as we read of all that he did for Israel in Old Testament times. We see our own need for a Savior and the impossibility of any system based on human merit.

Thus prepared, we turn to the New Testament, where we see the fulfillment of all that the Old Testament looked forward to and anticipated with eager longing, as we see God take on human form in Jesus. As we read, we not only learn about God, but we meet up with the God of grace who reveals himself through its pages.

Now it is possible to read the Bible many times and never see those things. It is possible to know the Bible by memory from cover to cover, and yet not experience any meeting up with God when we read it. Thus Paul speaks of those in his own day who read the Old Testament but failed to comprehend its true significance. It was as if a veil had been drawn over it, preventing them from getting to grips with what it was all about. Only in Christ was the veil taken away, enabling them to understand the matters of which it spoke (2 Cor. 3:14–15).

But the believer sees God with unveiled face in the Scriptures, and it is this unveiled vision of God that transforms us more and more into his likeness (2 Cor. 3:18). It is knowing the purity and love of God that makes us desire to be filled with a similar purity and love ourselves. It is seeing the loveliness of Jesus that gives us a hunger to live our lives after his pattern. It is understanding and believing that one day we will be with him and see him as he really is that motivates us to live purified lives here and now. As Paul puts it in 2 Corinthians 7:1,

> Since we have these promises, dear friends, let us purify ourselves from everything that contaminates body and spirit, perfecting holiness out of reverence for God.

It is meditating on the nature of God, as he is revealed in the Scriptures, and studying the promises of God, frequently and passionately, that drives us to desire a continually growing measure of present purity in our lives.

THE VISION OF GOD

After all, what is promised to us as the pure in heart is nothing less than that we will see God. Now if we tell our neighbor about that promise, the chances are he won't be very impressed. He'll say, "There you go again with your 'pie in the sky when you die' talk." But to adopt such an attitude is to denigrate the pie. This is not merely a passing pleasure. This is a pie that is worth waiting for. This is the fulfillment of that for which we were made.

We were created so that we might see God and live perpetually in his presence, just as Adam and Eve did in the Garden of Eden! What a privilege that will be! What an indescribable delight! For us to see as we are seen! For us to know as we are known! Isn't that worth whatever it may cost?

People have always been willing to give their lives for something they believed in passionately. A year ago a number of members of the Heaven's Gate cult committed suicide at Rancho Santa Fe, not far from where I live, in the belief that they would progress to a higher level of life aboard an alien spaceship lurking behind the Hale-Bopp comet. What was tragic about their end was not that they were sufficiently fanatical to be willing to die for something in which they believed. After all, Jesus himself said that anyone who wanted to follow after him should take up his cross. In those days a cross only had one purpose. It wasn't a cute decoration to hang around your neck. It was a particularly unpleasant instrument for killing people. To take up our cross and follow Jesus means nothing less than to be willing to die for the one who gave his life for us.

What was so tragic about the deaths of the members of the Heaven's Gate cult was that they were willing to give up their lives so cheaply. They sought simply to move on to the next level of evolution and see other intelligent life forms. What is to be envied about that?

But Jesus says, "Blessed are the pure in heart for they will see God." The idea will always seem nonsense to many, perhaps most people. They are much more concerned with how their friends see them than whether they will see God. But Christians are different.

Christians are passionately in love with the God who has so loved them first. They are irresistibly drawn to the One who demonstrated his love in sending Jesus to fulfill at such great personal cost all of the rich promises made throughout the Bible. They long therefore to be personally pure, with a purity that increasingly matches the purity of Jesus, which has already been credited to their account. They long to see God and thereby to be completely transformed into his likeness. Blessed indeed are the pure in heart.

FOR FURTHER REFLECTION

1. Why is a pure life particularly difficult in today's world?
2. How can you receive a pure heart?
3. What practical strategies have you found helpful in your pursuit of heart purity?
4. How can you feed and strengthen your longing for heart purity?

∽

SEVEN

THE
PEACEMAKERS

Blessed are the peacemakers, for they will
be called sons of God. (Matt. 5:9)

In each of our studies on the Beatitudes, we've started out by comparing and contrasting the attitudes Jesus tells us we are to have as Christians with the common attitudes of the world around us. Sometimes that contrast is easy to draw. The world is not unduly fond of righteousness and purity. But at other times the attitude Jesus is putting forward doesn't seem so radical after all.

So it is with this beatitude: blessed are the peacemakers. After all, who is against peace? We all want to live at peace, don't we? We want peace in our time on the global stage and an absence of conflict in our personal lives. We've even got the Nobel Peace Prize to reward those who go out of their way to promote international peace in a dramatic way. The pop singers similarly cry out, "All we are saying is give peace a chance." So who's against peace?

WHO'S AGAINST PEACE?

The answer is that we are all against peace, to some degree or other. What most people want is not peace but comfort. They simply want to experience an absence of conflict in their lives. They desire the opportunity to pursue life, liberty, and happiness without any hindrance. The world does *not* say, "Blessed are the peacemakers." It says, "Blessed are those who are comfortable and those who make our lives more comfortable."

In the Bible, however, peace is much more than the absence of conflict in our lives. In the Bible, peace involves right relationships with all those around us. Peace requires right relationships with both God and people. Peace is living together as a community in total harmony with God's laws.

What most of us long for is not so much peace as simply a quiet life. We want to be left alone. We reserve the right to say to others, "It's none of my business. It's your problem and I'm not going to bother myself about it. Leave me alone." We are not so much peacemakers as selfish comfort-seekers. Making peace, real peace, the kind of peace the Bible describes, goes thoroughly against the grain for all of us.

But if peace is difficult to make and if making it goes entirely against the grain, why should we seek to be peacemakers? Most people in the world only make peace when they think that they have something to gain by it. Look at most of the recent Nobel Peace Prize winners; most of them have some tangible benefit to gain, either personally or in terms of their community, from seeking peace. To be sure, they may have taken significant personal and political risks in the pursuit of peace, but they did so either for their own sake or for the benefit of their community. How are Christians different as peacemakers? What is it that motivates us to take the risky and often painful path of seeking to make peace?

GOD MADE PEACE FIRST

The first reason Christians are to be peacemakers is that God first made peace with us. Immediately, this reality moves us a step beyond where most people are. Unlike those who seek peace because they think it will make their lives more comfortable or because they stand to benefit from peace in some way, the Christian's impulse comes from the outside. The Christian's first motivation toward making peace springs not from self-interest but from something that has happened to her or him. God first made peace with us, so we also go out and make peace with others.

God's great peace-making work was accomplished at great personal cost, through the death of Jesus Christ. Listen to what Paul says in Ephesians 2:14–18:

> For he himself is our peace, who has made the two one and has destroyed the barrier, the dividing wall of hostility, by abolishing in his flesh the law with its commandments and regulations. His purpose was to create in himself one new man out of the two, thus making peace, and in this one body to reconcile both of them to God through the cross, by which he put to death their hostility. He

came and preached peace to you who were far away and
peace to those who were near. For through him we both
have access to the Father by one Spirit.

It is through Jesus that peace has been preached to us. More
than that, it is through Jesus' death that our peace has been accomplished. God has made peace for us not simply by means of
words but by means of radical actions. Unlike the creation of the
universe, which was in comparison a relatively simple affair, a mere
matter of speaking a few powerful words, achieving our peace required a much more costly involvement on God's part.

However, God's goal in redemption is not confined to making peace between ourselves and him. What he has done for us is
intended to affect radically the way we act toward one another. By
reconciling people first of all with himself, by taking people who
were his enemies and making them into his friends, God has at the
same time turned them from being enemies to one another into
friends to one another. Even longstanding divisions, such as the
wall between Jew and Gentile, are torn down through the redemp-
tive work of Christ. Notice the pattern here: God first made peace
with us; then, in so doing, he turns us into peacemakers and sends
us out to make peace with others.

JESUS, OUR PEACEMAKER

In all of this, Jesus himself is our model. He has the right to
tell us to be uncomfortable for the sake of making peace, because

he made himself uncomfortable for the sake of our peace. When we were lost in rebellion against God, by nature disinterested in him and not caring about him, he didn't say, "It's none of my business." He didn't say, "Saving these ungrateful little beings is their own problem. It's not worth the bother." He didn't say, "Never mind about them, leave me alone."

Now Jesus would have had a perfect right to say any or all of those things. We were in rebellion against him. We had decided that we could run our own lives. We were trying to live without him. Jesus knew that coming to earth would not only mean taking the form of a servant—how humbling for him, the one before whom every knee should bow! He knew that it would also mean offering up his body to mockery, scorn, and ultimately death on the cross, one of the most painful forms of execution ever invented.

But even that physical pain was not the worst of it. At his death, the debt of all of the sins of his people would be laid on him. Their iniquity would be charged to his account, and he would make payment for them all in full. Who can fathom how much that cost? Yet Jesus willingly paid that price in order that we might have peace with God, so that through his death we might become God's friends. In Jesus, God has demonstrated beyond a shadow of a doubt his commitment to making peace with us.

BEING PEACEMAKERS

But, as we've said, his purpose was not merely that we should be at peace with him. It was also that we should become peacemakers. If we are to be followers of Jesus, then other people's peace is necessarily our business. What, though, does that mean in practice? What does being a peacemaker involve for us?

To begin with, being a peacemaker involves doing our utmost to bring others into the same relationship of peace that we are now in toward God. If we are honest, most of us would have to admit that we find that very hard. We are often reluctant to share our faith with others, even when the opportunity presents itself.

Why are we so slow to talk to others? Well, we're tempted to say, "It's none of my business. What they believe is a private matter between them and God. It's not up to me to tell them what to believe." Now it is certainly true that we can't make people believe in God. But just as true, if we are going to be peacemakers, we cannot simply abandon them to their fate. We would have been lost forever if Jesus had waited for us to make the first move.

That means that with our friends at school, with our neighbors, with our workmates, the responsibility is ours to make the first move. We need to tell them about the peace we have found with God and about the difference God has made in our lives. We need to invite them along to visit church or to come to a Bible study. We must pray for them. We need to ask God to work in their hearts and bring them also to the point where they too will have peace with God. This is certainly not an easy task. It's not an assignment calculated to make us comfortable and popular. Not everyone will thank us for our interest in their peace. But Jesus doesn't say, "Blessed are the comfortable." He says, "Blessed are the peacemakers."

Being a peacemaker doesn't just mean trying to bring about peace between those around us and God, however. It also means trying to bring about peace between those around us and ourselves. As citizens of the kingdom, we must be at peace with our fellow-citizens. The apostle Paul therefore tells the Romans, "If it is possible, as far as it depends on you, live at peace with everyone" (Rom. 12:18). Paul means much more than "Don't go around picking fights." Some of us may think that we're living at peace with everyone simply because we don't fight with people. Look at the context of Paul's statement, however:

> Do not repay anyone evil for evil. Be careful to do what is right in the eyes of everybody. If it is possible, as far as it depends on you, live at peace with everyone. Do not take revenge, my friends, but leave room for God's wrath, for it is written: "It is mine to avenge; I will repay," says the Lord. On the contrary: "If your enemy is hungry, feed him; if he is thirsty, give him something to drink. In doing this, you will heap burning coals on his head." Do not be overcome by evil, but overcome evil with good. (Rom. 12:17–21)

The context given here is one in which someone is out to get us. Someone is picking on us. Whether it is at school or at home or in the workplace, whoever it is, they have hurt us and done wrong things against us. How are we going to respond to them?

It seems to me that we have three basic options, or ways of

responding. The first option is that we can get back at them. We can punch them out, or report them to the authorities, or put itching powder in their shoes—there are a thousand and one ways of doing it, if you are clever and creative enough. The motto of this option is "Fight fire with fire; repay evil with evil."

The second option is that we can refuse to respond at all. When they hit us, we just say nothing. We don't respond to their evil at all. The motto of this option is "Fight fire with a wet blanket."

Even this approach, which is often confused with peacemaking, is not enough for Paul. He wants us to consider a third option, that of overcoming evil with good. In other words, don't fight fire with fire; don't even fight fire with a wet blanket; rather, fight fire with an invitation to a barbecue. Return positive good for evil. That's what Paul means by being a peacemaker. That is the import of his statement "If it is possible, as far as it depends on you, live at peace with everyone."

Indeed, it is no more than Jesus said before him: "If someone strikes you on the right cheek, turn to him the other also. And if someone wants to sue you and takes your tunic, let him have your cloak as well. If someone forces you to go one mile, go with him two miles" (Matt. 5:40–41). The language is pictorial, and perhaps deliberately overstates the case to make the point—but don't use that as a reason to miss the point of what Jesus is saying! Christians are to go the extra mile in making peace. They are to do whatever is in their power to bring about peace between themselves and those around them.

This, of course, does not mean that we will never, ever

say anything that others find offensive. The same Jesus who told us to turn the other cheek also threw the moneychangers out of the temple. There will be times when, as Paul recognized, it is not possible to live at peace with those around us. The purity of the church and the honor and reputation of God may sometimes require us to make a stand for truth. However, our general reputation should not be as troublemakers, but as peacemakers.

STRENGTH FOR PEACEMAKING

Now if you're anything like me, you're feeling overwhelmed at this point. How can Jesus possibly expect us to be peacemakers if that is what it means to be a peacemaker? I don't have the strength to do it. Where are we to get the strength to live that kind of life? The clue comes in the second half of the beatitude: "Blessed are the peacemakers, for they will be called sons of God." Peacemakers will be called sons of God because they are displaying the family likeness.

Sometimes we say of a person, "Like father, like son," meaning that this person takes after his father in some particular way. Similarly, just as God is a peacemaker, so also his children will be peacemakers. What is more, it is precisely from the knowledge of their sonship that the strength to be a peacemaker comes. The Bible says that it is because we as Christians know ourselves to be God's sons that we have peace ourselves. Listen to how Paul puts it in Romans 8:14–16:

Those who are led by the Spirit of God are sons of God. For you did not receive a spirit that makes you a slave again to fear, but you received the Spirit of sonship. And by him we cry, "Abba, Father." The Spirit himself testifies with our spirit that we are God's children.

What this passage is saying is that when we become Christians, we become God's children. The result of that transformation in status is peace in our hearts with God. There is no more fear of being cast out; we are part of the family. This central biblical truth is what frees us to say, "What the world thinks about me doesn't matter. What my friends think about me doesn't matter. What I think about myself doesn't matter. Only what God thinks about me matters—and he has declared me one of his adopted children!"

In consequence, now I can go out boldly, confronting people where they need to be confronted, even if they hate me for it. I can humble myself and freely confess my own errors and sins, even if people don't respect me for it. I can love the unlovely, even though they don't love me in return. I can withstand the insults and assaults of others, without giving them back, because it is not what they think that counts. It is what God thinks that counts—and I have the assurance of his approval already.

Once again, we have a circular dynamic at work, just as we did with the beatitude about the merciful. There we said that Christians are those who have received God's mercy. The consequence of that is that they go out and show mercy to others, which makes them even more aware of their own need for mercy and thankful to God that mercy has been provided for them in Jesus Christ.

It is the same way with peacemaking: Christians are those with whom God has made peace through the power of the cross. They have been adopted into God's family. The result of that change is that they now go out and seek to bring others into God's peace and into peace with themselves. In so doing, they are imitating God, showing the family likeness, so that they will be called sons of God and will appreciate the privilege of peace with God all the more. They will not necessarily be called "the sons of God" by others; people may use quite different words to describe us. But that's not what counts! It is what *God* calls us that counts and in Christ he has declared us to be his children.

This pattern is repeated over and over in the Beatitudes. It's also a very important pattern in the growing Christian life. First God acts: he makes peace with us, he gives us purity, he shows us mercy, he gives us righteousness, he adopts us as his children. He makes the decisive move first. He brings about the legal change in our status, through what Jesus Christ did once and for all on the cross.

But we are not able to relax and kick back now because the legal change in our status has been made. Rather, we are to strive with every fiber of our being to become what we have been declared to be.

Have I been crucified with Christ? Then the life I live now, I must live entirely by faith in the Son of God (Gal. 2:20). Has God adopted you into his family? Then show the family likeness you profess: let peace flow out from you on all sides. Has God given you the purity of Jesus, freely credited to your eternal account? Then work to become purer in thought and deed, fixing your mind on whatever is true and noble and lovely. Has God shown you mercy? Then show mercy similarly to others. Has God given you a righteousness that is not your own? Then strive with all your being to live a life of matching righteousness by God's grace.

To be sure, we'll never outgrow our need for what God has done. Even our growth in grace itself is entirely purchased for us in Jesus' death on the cross. The work progressing in us remains God's work, and it progresses according to his timetable, not ours. So it is that we must go back time and time again to the cross for strength and for renewal of heart and mind, as well as for forgiveness when we fail. Then we plunge once more into the unending struggle to which God has called us, the struggle for peace, for purity, for mercy, for righteousness, and so on.

We strive and long with all our hearts to be what God has by grace declared us to be, and what he is making us to be as his Holy Spirit produces his fruit in us. In the meantime, we look forward to what we will one day be in completeness when God finishes his sanctifying work in us, fully at peace with God, with our neighbors, and with our world.

May our churches be places where peace is made. May they be places where peace is restored between God and men, women, and children. May they be places where peace is established between one person and another, transcending barriers the world's peace cannot surmount. May they be places where God's people are never too lazy or selfish to intervene, too tired or busy to go the extra mile, too self-protecting to turn the other cheek. May they be places where peace is preached to those who are afar off and those who are near and where peace is lived out among the community of God's children. Such communities of peacemakers will be known as the sons of God.

FOR FURTHER REFLECTION

1. Who are some well-known peacemakers? What is their motivation for pursuing peace?
2. Why is peacemaking so hard to do?
3. How did God make peace with you? How did you come to find out about this peace?
4. In what situations have you needed to seek peace with other Christians? How did you go about it? What advice would you give to others who are in similar situations?

❧

EIGHT

THOSE WHO ARE PERSECUTED

Blessed are those who are persecuted because of righteousness,
for theirs is the kingdom of heaven. Blessed are you when people insult you,
persecute you and falsely say all kinds of evil against you because of me.
Rejoice and be glad, because great is your reward in heaven,
for in the same way they persecuted the prophets
who were before you. (Matt. 5:10–12)

Once upon a time, a man was walking down a road when he saw another man pounding his head against a brick wall. Puzzled, the first man stopped walking and asked the other fellow why he was pounding his head against a brick wall. The other man replied, "I like to do this because it's so nice when you stop."

This, as you can imagine, is not a true story. I made it up, which would have been fairly obvious even had it not begun with "Once upon a time." For who but a masochist would do such a crazy thing? Which of us really likes to be hurt—even if it feels so good when the hurting ends?

Yet doesn't that seem to be the kind of thing that Jesus is saying here, when he says, "Blessed are those who are persecuted because of righteousness, because theirs is the kingdom of heaven"? Isn't Jesus really saying something like, "It's great to have your head pounded against a brick wall for the sake of the Lord because it will feel really good when it finally stops"?

Here, in the last of the Beatitudes, we have probably the most radical statement of them all. If each beatitude confronts the attitudes of the world, and confronts the attitudes of our hearts, then this one surely does so in triplicate. It takes our breath away with its boldness and leaves us asking if we can possibly live up to what it demands. What is so good about persecution that we should not merely admire but positively *envy* those who undergo it?

THE BLESSING OF PERSECUTION

The answer to that question is first of all to see precisely what it is that Jesus is saying. What he is saying is not that there is anything particularly good about persecution in itself, any more than there is in banging our heads against the wall. There is nothing necessarily sanctifying in being abused.

It is being persecuted *for the sake of righteousness* that Jesus particularly holds up as precious, not having people beating up on us for no reason at all. Thus, when he expands on this beatitude in verses 11 and 12, it is those who have people insult them, persecute them, and falsely say all kinds of evil against them *because of Jesus* who are blessed. In other words, the people we should envy and want to be like are those who suffer because of their commitment to Jesus.

This is the complete reverse of what the world says—and also of what we say in our hearts much of the time. The world says, "Blessed are those who live an easy life—even if the cost of that easy life means moral compromise." The world secretly (and sometimes not so secretly) envies people who cheat on tests and don't get caught, those who are able to shoplift candy without getting caught, those who are able to have affairs without their wives noticing—in short, people whose wickedness gets results.

The world admires people whose lives may be filled on the inside with contempt for God's standards and God's law, if on the outside they prosper and have easy lives nonetheless. The world is interested in studying the habits of effective people, not those of holy people. One of the world's "Ten Commandments" is this: "Thou mayest do whatever thou likest in pursuit of thine own comfort and happiness—and blessed art thou if it succeeds." So our magazines and TV programs are filled with lifestyles of the rich and famous, not with lifestyles of the totally committed and holy. If you must have a religion, the world just requires you to make sure that you find one that "works for you," fulfilling your needs and desires, whatever shape those aspirations take.

If we're honest, we have to admit that the same standard all too often applies to us. The bottom line for all of us too often boils down to the question "What's in it for me?" So we'll be peacemakers if we think that we have something to gain by it—but if not, then we'll try to exact our revenge. We'll be pure when and if it suits us—but if compromise seems to be likely to get us an easier and more en-joyable life, we'll compromise. We'll show mercy to people we like, but not to people who are continually making demands on us: that would only encourage them. We hunger and thirst less for what is right than for what feels good and looks attractive.

The result of this orientation is that we flee immediately from the slightest hint of persecution. We run away from the least opposition and bale out of any situation in which we feel uncomfortable.

But Jesus challenges us and our attitudes by saying, "Blessed are those who are persecuted for righteousness, for my sake." Why does he do that? What is it that persecution does for us?

PERSECUTION EXPOSES THE TRUE NATURE OF OUR FAITH

In the first place, persecution exposes the true nature of our faith. Where do we find out if we are Christians at all or merely cheap imitations? We find out in the fire of suffering for our faith. That's what the apostle Peter says:

> In this you greatly rejoice, though now for a little while you may have had to suffer grief in all kinds of trials. These have come so that your faith—of greater worth than gold, which perishes even though refined by fire—may be proved genuine and may result in praise, glory and honor when Jesus Christ is revealed. (1 Peter 1:6–7)

It's in the furnace that the stuff of which we are made is put to the test and demonstrated to be real—or false.

Last summer, my family and I visited Yosemite National Park. As we paddled in the Merced River, we noticed that the sand along the riverbed glittered with golden flakes. Knowing the gold mining heritage of the area, we might easily have been deceived into thinking that we had made a valuable discovery. However, if we had put those golden flakes into a crucible, we would have been disappointed with the end result, for the golden flakes were only "Fool's Gold," iron pyrites. They were not the real thing and an encounter with the furnace would have demonstrated that fact for all to see. Genuine gold is able to withstand the fire, but the dross is burned away. In a similar way, true faith is able to withstand persecution; imitation faith is destroyed by that kind of pressure.

Jesus makes the same point in the parable of the sower (Matt. 13:1–23). In that parable, the seed distributed by the sower fell onto four different kinds of soil. The first type of "soil" was the hardened ground along the path, where the seed had no impact at all. The second was the rocky soil, where the seed sprang up quickly but soon withered when the sun became strong. Then there was the thorny soil, where the seed was choked out by weeds. Finally, there was the good soil where the seed grew and prospered. Of particular interest to us at this point, though, is the second category of soil, the rocky soil. Listen to how Jesus interpreted the significance of the rocky soil:

> The one who received the seed that fell on rocky places is
> the man who hears the word and at once receives it with

joy. But since he has no root, he lasts only a short time. When trouble or persecution comes because of the word, he quickly falls away. (Matt. 13:20–21)

In other words, Jesus says it is possible to be a fake Christian. It is possible to look on the surface like a real Christian—just as iron pyrites looks like gold—but when the test comes, be exposed as a fraud. What, though, is the test that shows up the reality or otherwise of our faith? The furnace that puts our faith to the test is suffering and persecution. Indeed, if we manage to live our whole life without suffering or persecution, people will never really be able to tell if our faith is a reality in our hearts or merely the right words on our lips.

PERSECUTION REVEALS THE MOTIVES OF THE HEART

Now why is it that persecution and suffering act as the acid test of the genuineness of our faith? How do these things put our faith to the test? Quite simply, they reveal our true heart motives. In the midst of suffering and persecution, it becomes clear to ourselves and to others why we do the things we do. If our life progresses smoothly, with no challenges and no opposition, people may say, "It's easy for you to have faith. Look what an easy life you've had. You wouldn't still have that faith if you'd faced the challenges in life that I face." But if we have faced head-on persecution and difficulty, then people know—and we ourselves know—that we have a faith genuine enough to withstand the storm.

THOSE WHO ARE PERSECUTED

Let me illustrate that idea. When you marry someone, you promise that you will love your spouse "for better or worse, for richer or poorer, in sickness and in health." But as you are making that commitment on your wedding day, those are simply fine words. The promise is a good one and you believe that you mean it, but its reality has not been put to the test. On your honeymoon—at least in most cases—these are still only fine words. As long as everything remains for better, for richer, in health, the reality of your words has not really been tried. But when you discover her annoying habits and she discovers yours, when you discover that you are living with a fallen human being, not an angel in disguise, then you start to put a little reality into those words.

Still, it is only a little reality. It is not until it is substantially for worse, for poorer, or in serious, ongoing sickness, that you really expose for all to see whether your words were simply words, or if there is a heart reality underneath them. When he loses his job, or his ability to work, and plunges into deep despair—will you still love him then? When she turns out to have a wicked temper and a cutting tongue—will you still love her then? When he develops Alzheimer's disease and can't even remember your name? When she is confined to a wheelchair and you have to change her bedpan? Then, and only then, is the full reality—or otherwise—of your commitment to your spouse revealed. Did you marry this person so that she could meet your needs or so that you could meet hers?

The same principle is true of family: do you have children to meet your own needs or so that you can serve them? The way you find out is when the demands pile up.

This is particularly true when the demands are not just the usual childhood traumas—the sleepless nights and run-of-the-mill emergency room visits—but extend beyond that. When a child is born severely disabled physically or mentally and will require far more than the average self-sacrifice on the part of the parent, then the nature of the parental commitment is truly put to the test. When a child develops a long-term life-threatening condition that consumes the parent's time and resources, then the true nature of the parent's love is exposed. When teenagers rebel and refuse to conform to their parents' expectations, seeming instead to delight in humiliating their fathers and mothers, then the parents' hearts are laid bare for all to see.

The same reality is even true of churches. These days people often go to churches looking first of all to have their needs for friendship, teaching, and comfort met. Most people don't go asking where they can best use their gifts to serve the kingdom. They choose a church as a means to the end of meeting their felt needs rather than as a means to the end of serving God and his people. As long as a church measures up to their expectations, they will stick around, but should the church, or the pastoral staff, fail them in some way, then they are quickly off through the exit, in search of a "better" church.

Persecution and difficulty will inevitably tell the truth about our motivations. They reveal clearly whether we have made a Christian profession of faith because we want God to serve us or because, in response to the good news of the gospel, we want to serve God with a wholehearted commitment.

Are we really committed to God for better or worse, for richer or poorer, in sickness or in health? Are we using the world as a means to gain God or are we using God as a means to gain the world? As long as we can have both God and the world, it is going to be hard to tell for sure. But when we have to choose between God and the world, between serving God and progressing in our careers, between following God and getting married, between being rich to God and laying up large amounts of money, between obedience to God and life itself, then we find out in a hurry the true nature of our commitment.

PERSECUTION AS A BAROMETER OF FAITHFULNESS

As well as telling the truth about the reality of our faith, the extent to which we face persecution also often acts as a barometer of our faithfulness. Jesus says, "Rejoice and be glad when you are persecuted for righteousness because in the same way they persecuted the prophets who were before you." To put what Jesus says into other words, true prophets always tend to get themselves persecuted, while in contrast everybody typically speaks well of false prophets. That was true of Jesus himself, and it is true of his disciples. Remember what Jesus said in John 15:

> If the world hates you, keep in mind that it hated me first.
> If you belonged to the world, it would love you as its own.
> As it is, you do not belong to the world, but I have chosen

you out of the world. That is why the world hates you. Remember the words I spoke to you: "No servant is greater
than his master." If they persecuted me, they will persecute you also. If they obeyed my teaching, they will obey
yours also. (vv. 18–20)

To the extent to which our lives measure up to the standard
set by Jesus, to that same extent we can expect to be persecuted. If
we belong to the world—or if we act as if we belong to the
world—then no one will single us out for attention. If we swim
with the stream, we will never feel the force of the current. But
when we try to stand up against the current, we can expect to feel
the full weight of the stream against us.

What this means is that when we try to live up to the Beatitudes, we shouldn't expect everyone to applaud and cheer. If we
are purer than everyone else at work, and don't join in the dirty
jokes and mockery of God, then people will make fun of us. If we
are meeker than those around us, not insisting on our own
rights, people will try to take advantage of us. When we mourn
over sin, people will make fun of us and tell us not to be so old-
fashioned.

In this country, they may not take us out, stand us against a
wall, and shoot us, although there are countries around the world
where a faithful testimony may have that concluding chapter.
However, they will certainly insult us and falsely say all kind of evil
against us. The reality is that the more like Jesus we are, the more
we stand against the flow, the more persecuted we are likely to be.

REJOICING OVER PERSECUTION

It would be easy to feel depressed at this point, at the prospect of inevitable persecution accompanying faithful testimony. But Jesus doesn't want us to be depressed by persecution if we are Christians. He wants us to rejoice over it. Why should we rejoice at the thought (or present reality) of persecution? For precisely the reasons we have mentioned so far: persecution will demonstrate clearly and undeniably to all the reality and the essence of our faith.

Sometimes our attitude under persecution speaks to our persecutors and to the watching world far more loudly than any of our words could. When people see us standing firm, and not only standing firm but rejoicing in the face of opposition and suffering, they can't explain it. They can't account for it within their paradigm. In fact, the only explanation for such behavior is the reality of our faith and the reality of the God whom we serve.

As we are faithful under persecution, it is made clear that we are serving God not for anything we want to extract from him but simply out of love and gratitude for what he has done for us. It is one thing to *say* that we are entirely motivated in our service of God by love and gratitude for the gospel—and we should say that, loud and clear, just like a husband and wife should say "I love you" to one another often. But persecution and difficulty is where the rubber meets the road; these are the moments that demonstrate the reality underneath the words.

In addition, it is when we are suffering persecution for

the faith that we are most like Jesus. Paul's stated desire in Philippians 3:10 is this:

> I want to know Christ and the power of his resurrection and the fellowship of sharing in his sufferings, becoming like him in his death.

Many of us are familiar with that verse and perhaps even have it framed and hung on a wall in our home. Yet the "fellowship of Christ's sufferings" is nothing other than experiencing in some measure the same kinds of persecution and pains that he suffered, for the same goal: that men and women might be brought to faith in God and new life in Christ. To be sure, Christ's sufferings were unique in their atoning significance and power, but he calls us also to "take up our cross" and thereby share in the humiliation and pain that was poured on him for our sake and for the sake of the gospel.

THEIRS IS THE KINGDOM OF HEAVEN

Finally, steadfastness under persecution points clearly to our faith in the world to come. That's why Jesus says as the final motivation, "Theirs is the kingdom of heaven." The world hates suffering and persecution and avoids it at all costs because the world thinks only about this present existence. That approach makes sense if this world is all we have. If there is no prospect of heaven, then it is entirely reasonable to do whatever we can to avoid pain and suffering here on earth.

Christians, however, see beyond this world. They know that there is a reality to come that is far more wonderful than anything this life has to offer, a reality so wonderful that nothing they face in this world is too great a price to pay to attain the world to come. Eternal life in God's presence is the one thing that we must have at all costs. Let the world long for nice houses and fast cars, large bank accounts and comfortable lives; we long for something else. We long to stand before God and hear him say, "Well done, good and faithful servant. You have fought the good fight. You have demonstrated your faithfulness to me. Now come, enter into my joy."

As we end this book, we return to where we started in a sense, with the statement, "Theirs is the kingdom of heaven." That's where Jesus begins and ends the Beatitudes (Matt. 5:3, 10). There is the searching question that we have to answer: Do we want the kingdom of heaven? Do we want it more than we want anything else in the whole world? Do we want it more than we want our pride, more than our self-centeredness, more than our comfort, more than the cherished sins that we love so much, more than our desire for revenge, more than our ability to fit in?

If we are Christians, then the answer will be Yes! Yes, I love you, Lord, more than anything else. Yes, I want to be with you more than I want anything else. Yes, I want to see Jesus and to be filled with a purity and holiness that matches his purity and holiness. He is the true Christian hero. He is the one whose obedience and perfection have been credited to my account and enable me to be adopted into God's family, and whose obedience and perfection are to be progressively worked out through the work of the Spirit in my life. He is the one whose life I am to model my own after, no matter what the cost. By his grace, I too may be registered as a citizen of his kingdom. If I have that, then there is nothing else I need.

FOR FURTHER REFLECTION

1. How have you been persecuted for the sake of righteousness? How did you respond?

2. Can you think of some famous Christians whose witness under severe persecution speaks powerfully to the watching world?

3. How was Jesus persecuted? According to Hebrews 5:8, what fruit did such suffering bear in his life?

4. Why is persecution a good thing? Should we therefore seek out persecution?

5. How can you live a "kingdom of heaven focused" life and help others to do the same?

INDEX OF SCRIPTURE